INTRODUCTION

Welcome to the Open Learning Materials for New Deal for Musicians.

This set of workbooks has been developed for musicians and DJ's who are undertaking the Open Learning Route in New Deal for Musicians.

WHAT IS THE NEW DEAL FOR MUSICIANS?

The New Deal for Musicians aims to help musicians in the broadest sense, including vocalists, composers and performing DJ's. Many of these roles involve self employment and it is recognised that musicians need a flexible way of learning as their career progresses. These workbooks have been designed in a way that enables you to learn at your own pace, with help from your Music Open Learning Provider (MOLP) and with the ongoing mentoring support you can get from your Music Industry Consultant (MIC).

HOW WILL THESE MATERIALS HELP ME?

The music industry is very competitive, but if you are determined to succeed, there is a vast range of musical careers to choose from. These materials will help you to develop your skills and acquire a knowledge base that should enable you to work independently towards a career in the industry.

THE MUSIC INDUSTRY AND YOU

WORKBOOK 1

CHAPTER 1
HOW TO USE THE OPEN
LEARNING MATERIALS ⓔ

CHAPTER 2
HOW THE MUSIC
INDUSTRY OPERATES ⓔ

CHAPTER 3
SETTING
YOUR GOALS E

CHAPTER 4
NETWORKING E

HOW TO USE THE OPEN LEARNING MATERIALS

WHAT IS IT?

The Open Learning Materials are a set of nine workbooks, which help you move towards a career in the music industry. The workbooks are part of your MOLP programme, which will be designed specifically for you.

Your MOLP tutor will work with you to set your goals, decide which workbooks and chapters to study, decide what other tasks you need to do (for example, attending sessions in music technology, or rehearsing with your band) and check your progress.

WHY DO I NEED TO KNOW ABOUT THIS?

You need to read this chapter so that you get the most out of the materials.

Each workbook is a self-contained course, which you can work through at your own pace, with help from your MOLP.

You can 'mix and match' different chapters which are marked as 'Optional'.

Some chapters are marked 'Essential' which means these are the most important areas to study.

If you don't spend some time getting to know how these books work, you won't be able to get the full benefit from them.

INTRODUCTORY PLANNING EXERCISE

Start work on your Learning and Development Plan (LDP). Look at the contents of each workbook and decide which ones you think you need to complete first. (Read the Notes and Guidance section)

1. Look at the contents of each workbook and decide which ones you think you need to complete.
2. Put a tick next to the chapters you want to do.
3. Put two ticks next to the chapters which are MOST IMPORTANT to you.
4. Discuss your LDP with your MOLP
5. Add your other open learning goals into your main LDP, with the help of your MOLP, for example, rehearsing with your band, finding other musicians to work with, or writing material.

Ask for help from your MOLP to do this.

WORKBOOK	CHAPTER	IS IT FOR ME?	TICK HERE
WORKBOOK 1 essential **THE MUSIC INDUSTRY AND YOU**	Introduction to OLM	No project in this section	
	1. How to use the Open Learning Materials	You're learning this now!	
	2. How the Music Industry operates	The recording, publishing and live performance industries, who's who and how it all works.	
	3. Where now? Setting your goals	About you, where you're headed and how you can get there.	
	4. Networking	Who you need to know, why and how to do it.	
WORKBOOK 2 essential **WORK AND JOBS**	1. A Job in Music	About all the jobs in music, UK and abroad.	
	2. Skills, experience and training	How to get the skills you need.	
	3. How to find work and work placements	CVs, biogs, finding work, interviews.	
WORKBOOK 3 **CREATING**	1. Songwriting for rock and pop music	Understand your songs and make them better, with tips on music theory.	
	2. Creating music - Urban / Dance / R n B - Classical, Jazz, World - TV, film, games music	Understand and write the best music, including tips on music theory.	
	3. Remixing	Everything you need to know about remixing.	
	4. Arranging	Arrange your music for other styles and instruments.	
WORKBOOK 4 **PERFORMING**	1. Improving your skills: - Guitar / Bass - Piano / Keys - Vocals - Drums - DJ	How good are you? Different styles, genres, techniques to use.	
	2. Rehearsing	Get more out of your rehearsals.	
	3. Performing	The art of gigging and touring – musicians and DJs.	
	4. Health and Safety	What the law and other musicians say about health and safety.	
	5. Equipment	How to choose, maintain and repair your equipment for a price you can afford.	

WORKBOOK	CHAPTER	IS IT FOR ME?	TICK HERE
WORKBOOK 5 RECORDING AND PRODUCTION	1. Studio recording equipment	Getting started in a recording studio, using equipment to get the best results.	
	2. Music Technology equipment and software	Music Technology – getting started with the key equipment.	
	3. Production - Rock / Pop - Urban / Dance / R n B - Classical, Jazz, World - TV, film, games music	Get your demo together, with tips from producers.	
	4. Manufacture	How to get your product manufactured (small runs, design, packaging, duplication, web, CDR, DVD, MP3/MP4).	
5	5. Live Sound	Get the best sound – big and small, vocal and karaoke setups.	
WORKBOOK 6 MARKETING, PROMOTION DISTRIBUTION AND RETAIL	1. Why marketing, promotion and distribution?	Understand marketing, promotion and distribution.	
	2. Define your audience	Manager, Label, Publisher, Agent, Promoter, Public.	
	3. Creating and marketing your package	Market your product and yourself - getting gigs and finding venues.	
	4. Promotions	Radio, media, live events, publicity, sponsorship and merchandise.	
	5. Distribution	Where and how to distribute your product.	
6	6. Retail	Record shops, online, mail order clubs, digital downloads, music shops, pro-audio retail.	
WORKBOOK 7 COPYRIGHT, LEGAL AND MANAGEMENT	1. Dealing with intermediaries	Manager, accountant, lawyer – when do you need one?	
	2. What is copyright?	What copyright means - songs, sound recordings, publishing, clearance and infringement.	
	3. Music industry contracts	Recording, publishing, management, Agent / promoter / venue contracts.	
	4. Group agreements	If you collaborate with others, you've got to read this.	
7	5. Legal and business issues	Do's and Don'ts – how to survive in business – PAYE and tax	
WORKBOOK 8 BUSINESS AND MONEY	1. Dealing with financial advisers	Book keepers, accountants – when do you need one?	
	2. Preparing for self employment	Working for yourself – the real story. Includes business planning.	
	3. Exploitation of rights	Making music pay - how to get money from the music you create, play and record – PRS, MCPS and others.	
	4. The business of performance	Making money – from gigs, tours, merchandise.	
8	5. Money and earnings	Be Money Wise - Budgets, cashflow, funding. What do people earn?	
WORKBOOK 9 TEACHING MUSIC	1. A career in teaching music	Different teaching roles and how to do them.	
	2. Instrumental teacher	Musical and teaching skills, marketing and business plans for freelance work.	
	3. Community musician / music leader	Musical and workshop skills, marketing and business plans for freelance work.	
9	4. Schools and colleges teacher	Skills, experience and training – how to get what you need.	

WELL DONE, THAT'S THE END OF THIS ASSIGNMENT. CHECK IT AND HAND IT IN!

WHAT
do I do now?

HOW
will I be assessed?

HOW LONG
should this assignment take?

Every person works at his / her own pace. As a guide, this should take you 2 hours to read and research and another 2 hours to write your answers and discuss them with your tutor.

Your tutor will assess your work. He / she will give you feedback on how you have done. If you have not completed the work, you will be given the chance to do further work to bring it "up to scratch". For more details, please refer to your MOLP's own guidance.

Read the TASKS section below.
Then read the NOTES AND GUIDANCE section.
Carry out the TASKS.

TASKS

Read 'notes and guidance' to answer these questions

1 List 3 chapters from the workbooks which would be useful for someone wanting to organise a **GIG**.

1)

2)

3)

2 List 3 workbooks which would be useful for someone wanting to develop a career as a **SONGWRITER** or **COMPOSER**.

1)

2)

3)

3 Every chapter has the same sections. Tick the section where you would find information to help you complete the project.

☐ WHAT IS IT?

☐ WHY DO I NEED TO KNOW ABOUT THIS?

☐ PROJECT

☐ NOTES AND GUIDANCE

☐ WANT TO KNOW MORE?

4 Are you a library member? (If YES, skip this question) If NO, find out where your local library is and join it.

YOUR LOCAL LIBRARY

address

5 You will need to read music magazines, papers and books to do some of the projects in the workbooks. List some of the examples here:

Examples of music **MAGAZINES** :

Examples of music **BOOKS** or **DIRECTORIES** :

Examples of local **PAPERS** :

6 When you study, you need to spot important points. Read through the following paragraph and highlight the most important words, as if you were taking notes. Underline, circle or use a highlighter pen.

"An agent is responsible for booking all live appearances on behalf of the artist. The agent will normally be appointed by the manager. Commission is typically 15% of performance fee / ticket sales. An agent may work with many local promoters to set up a tour."

8 Carry out the following tasks using a computer.

→ Turn the computer on and open a word processing application (e.g. Microsoft Word) ☐

→ Using a word processing application, write a paragraph about yourself and save it to a disk, CD or hard drive of the computer. ☐

→ Print your work, then close the application. ☐

→ Open an Internet browser (e.g. Internet Explorer) and go to www.google.co.uk ☐

→ Shut down the browser and then the computer. ☐

9 Write your e-mail address here, or follow the instructions in Notes and Guidance on P121 to set up an account.

✉ My e-mail address is

10 Choose from these words below to complete the sentences accurately

15   30   9   Music Industry Consultant (MIC)   a selection of   MOLP tutor   NDPA (New Deal Personal Adviser)

QUESTIONS

1) My _____ will assess how well I am doing with the workbooks.

2) My _____ will give me general guidance and help me make contacts with other music industry people.

3) I need to prove that I have spent at least _____ hours per week in open learning.

4) I have a choice of _____ workbooks to study on MOLP.

11 LDP stands for

INTRODUCTION TO THE OPEN LEARNING MATERIALS

This section explains the design of the materials and how to use them properly.
Each workbook is a self-contained programme that helps you develop a career in the music industry.

HOW DOES THE PROGRAMME WORK?

You need to be active on the programme for at least 30 hours per week and record your activities in your diary, or on a time sheet, as your MOLP tutor tells you.

It's up to you and your MOLP tutor to decide the best way of using the 30 hours per week. You will need to have regular contact with your MOLP tutor, so you can:

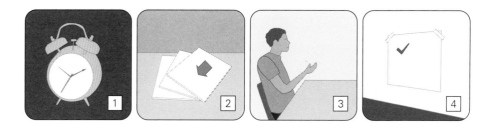

☐ 1

Decide what you need to be doing in your 30 hours per week, what you will achieve and by when.
– this might include writing your music at home, rehearsing or performing, or coming to classes, workshops or meetings at your MOLP.

☐ 2

Decide which workbooks and projects you need to be doing, what you will achieve and by when.

☐ 3

Get help and advice to do your work.

☐ 4

Check to see if you're doing what you have agreed and if you're making progress on the programme.

HOW TO STUDY

MOLP is designed to be flexible, so there is no single way of studying on the programme.
Here are two examples:

MOLP and Jon agree to do these things in the month before their next review or tutorial:

NAME JON
AGE 23

Jon is in a working band, playing regular gigs. He also writes and records his own material.
He has a manager, and is looking for a record deal.

ACTION POINTS FOR NEXT MEETING

Read and complete all of Workbook 1.

Read and complete chapter 1 of Workbook 2
- A Job in Music.

Read and complete chapter 4 in Workbook 6
- Promotions.

Rehearse new set for showcase gig next month.

Arrange and rehearse 3 chosen songs for new demo.

Select a recording studio with help from MOLP tutor at next meeting.

Start to work on budget for showcase gig.

MOLP and Yvonne agree to do these things in the month before their next review or tutorial:

NAME YVONNE
AGE 19

Yvonne is a beginner level DJ. She has a small collection of records, with a basic set of decks at home. She has played at friends' parties, but needs to get some paid work.

ACTION POINTS FOR NEXT MEETING

Read and complete all of Workbook 1

Read and complete chapter 3 of Workbook 2
- How to find work and work placements.

Read and complete chapters 3 and 5 of Workbook 4
- Performing and Equipment.

Attend a taught session organised by your MOLP with a guest DJ tutor.

Prepare your set list for a gig and make a demo recording onto minidisk.

ATTENDANCE

Jobcentre Plus has strict rules about attendance and good timekeeping on all programmes, including MOLP. **For MOLP, this means carrying out at least 30 hours of activities per week, as agreed with your tutor.**

YOU NEED TO

Attend for reviews or tutorials, seminars or other sessions which your tutor tells you to.

Fill in your diary as you make progress, with at least 30 hours of work each week.
Your tutor will tell you about attendance requirements. If you don't attend, then you will be dismissed from the programme – ask for a copy of your attendance policy.

CHOOSING YOUR WORKBOOKS

1 SPEAK WITH YOUR MOLP ADVISER

During your induction, your MOLP adviser will issue you with workbooks 1 and 2. Look at the Project in this chapter with your adviser. It shows you to how to start work on your Learning & Development Plan.

2 SELECT THE CHAPTERS that you need to study.

We recommend that everyone studies workbooks 1 and 2.

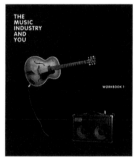 

Remember – each chapter contains a Project, which is a series of tasks, questions and exercises for you to complete. It's really important to complete the Project, as it is the tool by which you learn more about your subject.

Look at the project on P11-14 for a full list of all the chapters.

LINK IN WITH YOUR MOLP ADVISER

Your MOLP adviser is your key contact as you use the workbooks.
He/she will monitor your progress, give you help, support and assistance and assess your work.
Your New Deal Personal Adviser will also contact you to check on progress during your programme.

ABOUT THE WORKBOOKS

The new Open Learning Materials have been developed as a set of 9 workbooks, together with a diary.
You will find more details of all the workbooks, chapters and projects in the Project for this chapter.
Some of the chapters in each workbook are ESSENTIAL. They contain vital information and tasks.
Other chapters are OPTIONAL.
You can decide with your MOLP adviser which optional chapters you are going to do.

THE WORKBOOK CHAPTERS

Each chapter inside the workbook is structured in exactly the same way, so it's easier to use.

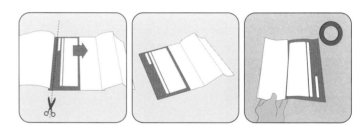

1

WHAT IS IT?

Tells you what the chapter is about

3

PROJECT

A list of tasks or questions for you to complete, within a given time.
These help you learn new skills, prove your understanding and create evidence for yourself and your tutors that you are progressing on the programme.

2

WHY DO I NEED TO KNOW ABOUT THIS?

Tells you how this will help your music career

As well as the section  - ,
each workbook contains:

CASE STUDIES
These are short stories or anecdotes about people who work in various areas of the music industry, telling you about aspects of their work and hopefully giving you some pointers.

TIP (marked as TIP **)**
Tips from seasoned industry professionals.

4

NOTES AND GUIDANCE

The information you need to carry out the project.
This section can be quite large, but by following
the headings in the contents sheet, you can find your
way around.

5

WANT TO KNOW MORE?

This section has 2 areas:

1. Web links, Books and Magazines
to help you through your tasks and to find out more
about the subject.

2. More tasks
to give those with more experience, or with a
particular interest in the subject, the chance to
explore further

Will my progress be monitored?

Where does my MIC fit in?

Can I jump from one workbook to the other?

How long will it take me?

Your Learning and Development Plan, which you develop with your MOLP adviser, is the plan for working through the course. Your progress will be monitored as you work through the materials and complete the Projects.

You will also continue to be able to contact your Music Industry Consultant for advice and guidance during New Deal.

The workbooks all follow roughly the same format and design, making it easy for you to jump from one to the other. There are plenty of signposts (≫) which point you to other relevant sections in different workbooks. There are also icons to help you identify the various music genres covered.

The idea behind open learning is that you can learn independently at your own pace. The books are designed in a way that encourages and motivates you to find out more about the music industry. Some chapters will take longer than others to complete, but it's usually around 4-6 hours.

POP/ROCK

URBAN/R'N'B/DANCE/DJ

CLASSICAL/JAZZ/ROOTS

COMMERCIAL/FILM AND TV

What evidence will I have of my progress?

All the projects involve answering questions or completing tasks.
The projects will enable you to measure your progress.
You can use this evidence when applying for work, work experience, or perhaps to move onto other courses.

How will I be assessed?

Your tutor will assess your work. He / she will give you feedback on how you have done. If you have not completed the work, you will be given the chance to do further work to bring it "up to scratch". For more details, please refer to your MOLP's own guidance.

Can I gain a qualification just by completing the workbooks?

No. The Open Learning Materials are not accredited at present. However, your MOLP may have a qualification which you can work towards – ask your tutor for more information.

What do I do if I have difficulty in completing the work?

You might need extra help if you

- Find it difficult to complete paperwork

- Struggle with numbers and maths

- Struggle with reading or writing

- Have a disability or health problems

Speak to your tutor first, who will help you find a solution. You can also speak to your Jobcentre Plus Personal Adviser.

What happens if I disagree with an assessment?

Speak to your tutor first. If you still disagree, then ask for a copy of the appeals procedure which will tell you how to appeal.

Basic computer literacy

You will need basic computer skills to complete parts of the project. If you can't complete the tasks in Question 8, you need to improve your skills. Speak to your tutor and agree what steps you have to take. This may include:

- Enrolling on a basic computer course

- Using tutorials or help files in software such as 'Word'.

- Using tutorials such as 'www.tutorials.com'.

How to start your Learning and Development Plan (LDP)

Read through the Project question called "Introductory Planning Exercise" in this chapter. You can start to create a Learning and Development Plan by selecting various chapters from the workbooks.

STUDY SKILLS

Don't be afraid to ask for some help from your MOLP – many people on New Deal for Musicians have been out of education for some time and need to refresh their skills.

READING SKILLS

Preview what you're going to read – title, chapter heading, any 'blurb' on the front or back of a book, these all help you decide how relevant it will be. Is it up to date? Check the date of the publication (usually on the inside of the front cover, or you might be able to see when a website was last updated).

Skim reading – cast your eye over a paragraph to pick up any important (key) words, before deciding if it will be useful to read more thoroughly.

Reading on screen – is hard on your eyes! Adjust the size of the document or the size of print to help you. Always remember to save things which you will want to look at again, or even print them out.

Lighting – make sure you read in good, strong light. If you don't, your eyes will get tired and you will lose concentration more easily.

Make notes – when you find information which you know is relevant and which you will want to use, take notes and also make a note of where you found the information.

TAKING NOTES

Prepare – planning is important. Take a pen and paper with you. If you can, read up about the subject beforehand. Make a note of any questions you want to get answers to. Make sure that the book you want is in the library, or that you've booked time on the Internet before you go.

Listening - if you're taking notes whilst someone is talking, you need to be able to listen to the important points, not spend your time writing down everything that is said. Sit where you can hear and see well.

Taking note of the important points – look out for chapter headings, or leading paragraphs at the top of a web site page. Watch out for words which signify an important point, such as 'most importantly' or 'particularly' or 'key'.

Taking notes – you can make notes on paper or in a notebook, or in the margins of your workbook. Underline or highlight important points. Use bullet points and abbreviations. Make an exact note of the book, magazine, website or other source of your information. Note down: Author - Title - Publisher - Date - Page

ORGANISING

Try using envelope folders (cardboard), all marked with separate headings.

Keep your project work safe within a plastic cover.

Write your name on your folders and notes.

Label CDs or other storage devices you use on the computer.

Always keep copies when possible and ALWAYS keep a copy of your project work.

Use a diary, or your mobile phone to keep track of important information.

Clear out your e-mail account regularly, saving essential e-mails in an archive folder.

Use the wallet at the back of the workbook to help you store your notes.

Use your diary!

FINDING INFORMATION

Use your library
Find out where your local and main libraries are.
You can join a library where you live, work, or study, free of charge.
Ask your librarian to show you how to use the catalogue / index system. It will probably be on computer and easy to use.
Learn how to use the classification system in libraries, where books on a certain subject are all in the same place. Within that place, the books will be in alphabetical order.

Talk to people
People are an easy source of information. You can usually get a relevant answer very quickly. People will also be able to point you in the right direction to find the information.
You can also find information which is useful, but which you didn't think to ask for.
Use open questions "what do you think is the best way to get a gig?" or "what suggestions would you make?" to get a range of information and to open up conversation.
Use closed questions "do you have any vacancies?" or "are you going to that gig tonight?" to find answers to specific questions and to tie a person down to one answer.

HOW RELIABLE IS YOUR INFORMATION?

Check Internet sources carefully. If possible take your information from more than one place.

Check that your information is relevant to the UK (or whatever region you are looking for). Different rules and laws may apply, for example, in Scotland, Wales and Northern Ireland. USA information is not always relevant to the UK.

How up to date is your information?

Is your information factual or someone else's opinion?

PLACES TO LOOK FOR INFORMATION

1 Gig listings, flyers
    Keep in touch with other bands and musicians. Making new contacts.

2 Local 'what's on' guide
    Explore any new venues that are opening.

3 Local newspaper adverts and features
    Watch how other use the media to develop their career

4 Telephone directories
    Finding contacts

5 TV and radio programmes
    Keeping abreast of the national scene

6 The Internet
    Making new contacts through discussion groups and newsgroups. Finding new products

7 Music shops
    Talking to other musicians.
    Watching new developments.

8 National music papers and magazines
    Keeping abreast of the national music scene. Reading adverts for musicians. Reviews of the latest music.

WANT TO KNOW MORE?

LINKS

New Deal for Musicians has no responsibility for or control of the following sites. The inclusion of any site does not necessarily imply New Deal for Musicians approval of the site. To access any of the sites please type in the address into a browser or search using keywords from the name of the link.
www.dfes.gov.uk/ukonlinecentres Find Internet access that's close to you.

INFORMATION ABOUT NEW DEAL AND NEW DEAL FOR MUSICIANS

☐ **www.newdeal.gov.uk**
Jobcentre Plus website on New Deal, follow the links for New Deal for you or search in the site. General information.

☐ **www.newdeal.gov.uk/documents/musicians/NDL51.pdf**
The New Deal for Musicians leaflet on-line

☐ **www.scottishculture.co.uk/ndfm**
Scotland's New Deal for Musicians site, good general information with suggested links for Scottish NDFM clients, from Scotland's MIC service.

☐ **www.citycol.com/ndfm**
NDFM site for Manchester, hosted by the Music Industry Consultants at City College Manchester. Hundreds of links to local promoters, venues etc plus information which is useful across the UK, such as funding advice for musicians.

☐ **www.delni.gov.uk**
Northern Ireland's Department for Employment and Learning
– look under New Deal for information on New Deal for Musicians

INFORMATION ABOUT CLAIMING BENEFITS, LOOKING FOR WORK AND JOBCENTRES

☐ **www.jobcentreplus.gov.uk**
Jobcentre Plus main website

☐ **www.dwp.gov.uk**
Department for Work and Pensions. Access to information about benefits, jobcentres

☐ **www.adviceguide.org.uk**
Citizens Advice website with advice on benefits, employment and a range of other topics such as debt and legal rights.

TIPS ON STUDYING

☐ **www.support4learning.org**

☐ **www.bbc.co.uk/learning**

USING COMPUTERS TO HELP WITH THIS COURSE

☐ **www.nailitnow.com.au/word**

☐ **www.learnthat.com/courses/computer**

☐ **www.intelinfo.com/office.html#word**

MUSIC MAGAZINES
TO BUY OR READ ON-LINE

☐ **www.q4music.com**
Q Magazine
U.K. music magazine. Includes reviews and industry news, plus details of the annual Q Awards.

☐ **www.kerrang.com**
Kerrang. Influential and widely read Rock magazine.

☐ **www.nme.com**
NME. Large distribution music newspaper

☐ **www.billboard.com**
US based music magazine

☐ **www.mojo4music.com**
Mojo Magazine. Online version of the U.K. music mag featuring reviews, news, buyer's guides, features, classified, and more.

☐ **www.thewire.co.uk**
Covers avant rock, breakbeat, jazz, modern classical, electronica, and other sounds from the outer limits.

☐ **www.gramophone.co.uk**
Gramophone. Classical music magazine with monthly reviews, Gramophone Awards, Editor's Choice, and more.

☐ **www.opera.co.uk**
OPERA. UK magazine with news, reviews and a diary section giving listings for all major opera-houses and forthcoming season programmes.

☐ **www.sospubs.co.uk**
Sound On Sound. Highly rated music technology / recording based magazine.

☐ **www.djmag.com**
DJmag. Covers dance music and club culture in the U.K.

☐ **www.djtimes.com**
monday, july 5 2004. International magazine for professional mobile and club DJ

☐ **www.mobilebeat.com**
Mobile Beat : The DJ Magazine

☐ **www.jockeyslut.com**
Jockey Slut. DJ and cutting edge music magazine

☐ **www.mixmag.net**
Mixmag. DJ Magazine

☐ **www.froots.demon.co.uk**
Folk Roots. UK based Traditional music (folk, world) magazine. Includes full UK / European festival listings.

☐ **www.musicweek.co.uk**
Music Week. The essential UK music business news.

MORE TASKS

1 Investigate more about New Deal options –
   1) How do you get a New Deal mentor?
      Ask your New Deal Adviser who provides mentoring and how you get in touch.
   2) Ask about the Adviser Discretionary Fund, what it's for and how you can apply.
   3) What happens at the end of your programme on MOLP?
      Ask your tutor and your NDPA, or look on the Jobcentre Plus website.
   4) What is test trading and who can do it?

2 Investigate extra sources of information while you're on the programme
   1) Do you have a MIC (music industry consultant)? If not, why not find out their details from your MOLP tutor and ask your New Deal Adviser about it.
   2) Contact and meet other NDFM clients and ex-clients who are working towards similar goals and workbooks. You can share ideas, contacts and work together or exchange emails about difficult areas of the programme.

3 How good are your study skills? Read the following paragraph and highlight the 'key points'. Either underline them or use a highlighter.

It isn't easy to get started in the music or other cultural industries.

The sector contains so many different organisations – record companies, production companies, publishers, publicists and so on – that it's hard enough to work out how it all fits together, let alone find a way in. Moreover, getting started is only the first step; to survive as a musician or performer you need to be multi-skilled, flexible and entrepreneurial.

You will almost certainly have to work as a freelancer or on short-term contracts, and will need enough drive and determination to create your own opportunities for work. You will also need good administrative skills and knowledge of marketing, promotion and funding systems.

4 Take notes from someone talking.
This might be from a lecture, a meeting or a discussion. If you don't know where to start, try to take notes from a radio news bulletin. It's harder than you think!
   1) make a note of topic headings and key points
   2) take down any names or facts which seem important (check spelling afterwards)
   3) summarise, don't write every word
   4) make a list of questions left unanswered at the end

HOW THE
MUSIC
INDUSTRY
OPERATES

WHAT IS IT?

This chapter explains how the music industry operates and how you can use the Internet to find out more about it.

We will look at the three main 'revenue streams' from music...

RECORDING
PUBLISHING
LIVE PERFORMANCE

... and your immediate team of business advisers around you.

We will look at the businesses, both large and small, that operate within these areas of music, such as record labels, publishers, promoters and managers.

We will look at some of the organisations that represent the interests of writers, performers, managers, producers, publishers and labels.

We will look at the 'collection societies' that collect royalties on behalf of writers, performers and producers.

Importantly, we will look at ways of FINDING information about the music industry, by using the INTERNET.

WHY DO I NEED TO KNOW ABOUT THIS?

As a musician, performer, DJ or producer, it is entirely understandable that your primary focus will be making and performing music to be proud of. It is not realistic, however, to believe that talent is all you will need to be successful in the music industry.

In music, everyone needs to have a good team around them. It is therefore crucial for you to become familiar with the 'big picture' of how the music industry operates, so that you can start to find out where you fit into it.

Then you can start the process of networking and action planning to help you reach your goals.

As you read through this and other workbooks, your knowledge and confidence will grow.

1) Find a **LOCAL** or **NATIONAL MUSIC, THEATRICAL** or **DJ AGENCY.**

Who are they?

Where are they?

How many artists do they represent?

Does it say how much commission they charge?

TIP

Try yellow pages for local ones

3) Find a **NATIONAL CONCERT PROMOTER.**

Who are they?

Give these examples of the type of concerts that they promote.

TIP

Look in the back pages of national newspapers

9 Using the Internet, find and research the following:

Who looks after the interests of independent record labels in the UK?

Which organisation looks after the interests of musicians in the UK?

Use this site (www.bmr.org) to find out more about the industry if you are a writer or performer.
Write two new facts you have discovered.

1

2

2) Find a **LOCAL MUSIC PROMOTER** in your area, who puts on gigs, club nights or other events.

Who are they?

What type of event do they promote?

4) Find a small or medium sized **LIVE MUSIC** or **CLUB VENUE** in your area.

Name of venue?

What is the capacity of the venue?

Give 3 example of music events that take place there.

1

2

3

TIP

Try local venues

10 Using the Internet, find and research the following:

Find out more about one of the following trade fairs: MIDEM, SXSW, Popkomm, Miami Winter Music Conference.

Which trade fair have you researched?

Where and when does it take place?

What kind of music does it cater for?

How much does a delegate pass cost?

WELL DONE, THAT'S THE END OF THIS ASSIGNMENT. CHECK IT AND HAND IT IN!

5 Put these in order of size, starting with the biggest – which countries buy the most recorded music?

Germany **1**

UK **2**

Japan **3**

USA **4**

6 Using the Internet or another way, find and research two music publishers.

1) Find a LARGE "MAJOR" MUSIC PUBLISHER

Who are they?

Where are they based?

What kind of music do they publish?

Name one writer who is on their roster

Do they have a website? What is it called?

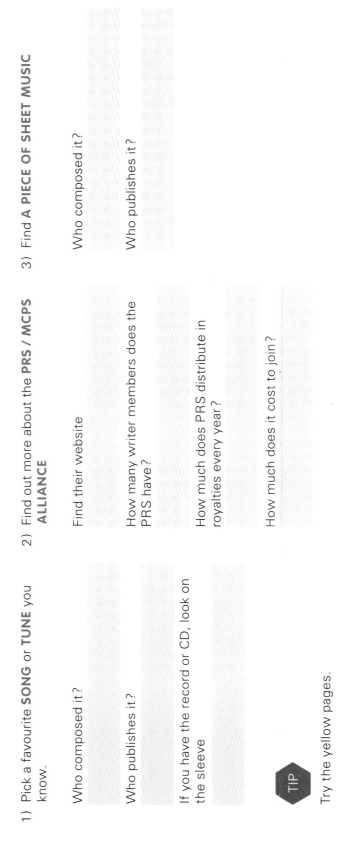

TIP

Search for the major record companies

2) Find a SMALL "INDEPENDENT" MUSIC PUBLISHER

Who are they?

Where are they based?

What kind of music do they publish?

Name one writer who is on their roster

Do they have a website? What is it called?

TIP

Try the Music Publishers Association

7 Using the Internet or another way, find and research the following

1) Pick a favourite SONG or TUNE you know.

Who composed it?

Who publishes it?

If you have the record or CD, look on the sleeve

TIP

Try the yellow pages.

2) Find out more about the PRS / MCPS ALLIANCE

Find their website

How many writer members does the PRS have?

How much does PRS distribute in royalties every year?

How much does it cost to join?

3) Find A PIECE OF SHEET MUSIC

Who composed it?

Who publishes it?

WHAT
do I do now?

Read the TASKS below.
Then read the NOTES AND GUIDANCE section
Carry out the TASKS.

HOW
will I be assessed?

Your tutor will assess your work. He / she will give you feedback on how you have done. If you are not able to complete the work, you will be given the chance to bring it "up to scratch". For more details, please refer to your MOLP's own guidance.

HOW LONG
should this assignment take?

Every person works at his / her own pace. As a guide, this should take you 10 hours to read and research and another 3 hours to write your answers and discuss them with your tutor.

TASKS   Read 'notes and guidance' to help you answer these questions

1   Read these words - tick which part(s) of the music industry they belong in.

	RECORDING	MUSIC PUBLISHING	LIVE PERFORMANCE	write any **NOTES** here
Distributor				
Promoter				
Merchandise				
Performance Fee				
PRS royalty				
Record label				
Songwriter				
Roadie				
Manager				
Remixer				
Rapper				
DJ				
Turntablist				
Recording artist				
Covering a song				
Licensing				
Agency commission				
Recording studio				
Sound engineer				
PA system				
MCPS				
I write music				
I record music				
I perform music				

2   Use words from this list to complete the following sentences: Manager   Accountant   Lawyer   Commission

Someone who professionally represents the business interests of an artist is called a _____ .
They take a _____ of around 20% and may work with a _____ to help negotiate recording and publishing deals.
Financial statements and tax returns will be prepared by the _____ .

3 Using the Internet or another way, find and research three record labels

1) SMALL RECORD LABEL
Find a local Indie label

Who are they?

Where are they based?

What kind of music do they put out?

Name one artist who is on their roster

Do they have a website? What is it?

2) MEDIUM SIZED RECORD LABEL
Find a large Indie label based in London

Who are they?

Where are they based?

What kind of music do they put out?

Name one artist who is on their roster

Do they have a website? What is it?

3) MAJOR RECORD LABEL

Who are they?

Where are they based?

What kind of music do they put out?

Name one artist who is on their roster

Do they have a website? What is it?

---

4 Using the Internet or another way, find and research the following

1) Find a local RECORDING STUDIO

Who are they?

Where are they based?

What is their hourly rate?

What equipment do they have?

TIP

Try the yellow pages.

2) Find a DISTRIBUTOR

Who are they?

Where are they based?

Name one label that they work with

TIP

Look for the distributor on the back of records or get hold of a copy of Music Week

3) Find two types of RETAILER
- A local record shop
Who are they?

What type of music do they retail?

- An online digital download shop
Who are they?

What type of music do they retail?

4) Pick a favourite RECORDING ARTIST or DJ / REMIXER

Who is their record label?

Who is their publisher?

Who is their manager?

TIP

Find their website using 'Google'.

HOW THE MUSIC INDUSTRY OPERATES

THE MUSIC BUSINESS IS
JUST THAT... A BUSINESS!

Over the next few pages we
will look at how money is
made from recording, music
publishing, live music
performance and all their
related businesses. We will
look at how those businesses
work, and you will hopefully
begin to see where you fit in!

Let's start with the basics. If
you are writing, recording or
performing music in any way,
there are three ways of
making money.

photography Ray Chan

RECORDING

If you have made a sound recording and sell it in any way, you are in the recording industry!
There are a number of ways of doing this:

If you are a recording artist, you will make a record for your record label, who then manufactures CD's and sells them in shops, by mail order or even on the Internet. You will get paid a royalty for every record you sell.

Alternatively, you could look for a distributor yourself, who will get the records into the shops for you. You take a bigger cut, but you have to do a lot more work.

On a smaller scale, you can duplicate your own CD's and sell them at the back of gigs, through local record shops, or even by digital downloads on the internet.

You could create MP3 files and 'license' your recordings to a digital download site, who will sell them on your behalf.

You can also license your recordings to other labels or on compilation albums.

If you are a producer or remixer, you get paid a fee for helping to create that recording, and you may even share in some of the profits.

What is actually being bought and sold, is the rights (or copyright) to the sound recording. More information in workbooks 7 and 8.

You make money when other people use your music to make recordings, perform on radio, television or at gigs.

You make money when someone else covers your music – i.e. they make a recording from it or perform it live to a large enough audience.

You make money when your music is performed on radio / TV, or when someone uses it on a film, TV programme or even a computer game.

The business people you have to deal with are called publishers. They help to exploit your music and make money out of it.

You can receive royalties from the performance and recording of your music through collection societies such as the PRS and MCPS. WORKBOOK 8 – CHAPTER 3

What is actually being bought and sold, is the rights (or copyright) to the music and lyrics. More information in WORKBOOK 7 and 8.

PUBLISHING

If you have written a song, lyrics, or any piece of original music which you sell, then you are in the publishing industry!

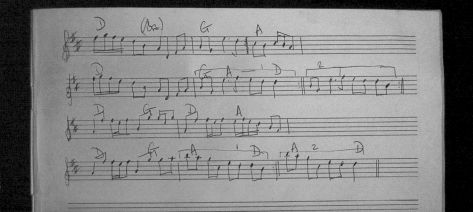

LIVE PERFORMANCE

If you get paid to perform music as a musician, performer or DJ, then you are in the live performance industry!

If you are a performer, then you will probably receive a fee for performing.

A professional cabaret artist will receive a straight fee.

A DJ will probably receive a straight fee.

An established touring artist may receive a share of the box office takings as well.

There is also merchandising to think about. Gigs offer opportunities to sell T Shirts and other stuff with your name on it.

The business people you have to deal with are called **AGENTS** and **PROMOTERS**.

AGENTS get paid a commission to book the artists.

PROMOTERS take the financial risk on the concert by paying for the venue, advertising and the artist in advance. They take the biggest risk, so they often get the biggest reward.

If you are an artist, you will also come into contact with important business advisers and other businesses. These are...

ARTIST

LAWYER

MANAGER

ACCOUNTANT

THE MEDIA
(PRESS / RADIO / TV)

ROUTE 1
RECORD COMPANY

A&R
MARKETING
BUSINESS AFFAIRS
PROMOTION

ROUTE 2
PUBLISHING COMPANY

A&R
ROYALTY TRACKING
PROMOTION

ROUTE 3
LIVE PERFORMANCE

A&R
PROMOTER
TOUR MANAGER
MERCHANDISE

SALES & DISTRIBUTION

RECORD SHOPS

OTHER RETAILERS / MAIL ORDER

THE INTERNET

COLLECTION SOCIETIES

LIVE VENUES

**THE MEDIA
(PRESS / RADIO / TV)**

THE PUBLIC

MANAGEMENT TEAM

The **MANAGER** represents the artist in all business environments and interests. The manager will negotiate ALL contracts in collaboration with the artist and with advice from his / her business advisers (lawyer and accountant). Generally takes around 20% (gross) of all monies earned – this is called a commission. (More in workbooks 6 and 7)

The **LAWYER** (typically a specialist music lawyer) is responsible for advising the manager and artist on all offers / contracts. (More in workbooks 7 and 8)

The **ACCOUNTANT** is required to prepare financial statements and annual tax returns and oversee all transactions. (More in workbooks 7 and 8)

TIP

Need to find yourself a manager? Go to ≫ WORKBOOK 7

THE RECORDING INDUSTRY

Now lets look at the three 'revenue streams' in more detail.
The recording industry makes money by exploiting the rights to sound recordings that it owns. In practical terms, this means that it makes money by selling recordings. (See workbook 7 for more information)

Here are the component parts of the recording industry.

RECORDING ARTIST

The artist who performs on the recording. They may actually write the music too, **but not always**. The recording artist is generally signed 'exclusively' to the record label. This means that the artist can not record for another label without permission.

PRODUCTION

This is the recording studio, engineer, session musicians, producer and technical staff who create the sound recording.

RECORD COMPANY / LABEL

The record label pays for the sound recording to be made and the marketing costs to advertise and promote it. They sign the recording artist to a **recording contract** which stipulates that the artist must record 'exclusively' for them. **A&R** (Artist and Repertoire) is the department that finds the talent and nurtures and develops it.

MANUFACTURE

Manufacturing has been traditionally done by **pressing plants**. Large pressing plants can produce hundreds of thousands of CDs a day. Some recording studios have their own duplication facilities for 'small runs'. Pressing on demand is the key to producing the optimum amount needed to meet pre-sale orders and predicted sales on a regional and national basis. With **digital distribution** on the Internet, pressing plants are not required, as the music is delivered electronically through telephone lines, mobile phones and the Internet.

DISTRIBUTION

The **distributor** receives the product from the manufacturer, who then warehouses all the recordings and gets them into the shops. With **digital distribution** on the Internet, there are new kinds of distributors who will put your music on the web and manage all the electronic transactions for you.

RETAIL

The final **point of sale** to the consumer. This could be a record shop, a book club, mail order, supermarket or an online retailer. With **digital distribution**, you can buy the digital sound files directly on the web with an electronic payment. This is becoming increasingly popular. The sales figures in a relatively small number of record shops are used to generate the weekly Top 40 charts. There are now 'download' charts too.

WHAT'S IT WORTH?

The UK recording industry is worth billions of pounds.
Consumers spend around **£3 billion** in total on music and spend about **4 hours a week** on average listening to recorded music.

It is estimated that UK artists have a **15% share** of the world music market.
The UK exports twice the amount of music it imports

WHO BUYS THE MOST MUSIC IN THE WORLD?

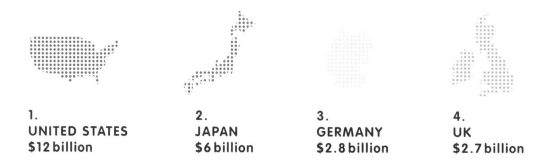

1.
UNITED STATES
$12 billion

2.
JAPAN
$6 billion

3.
GERMANY
$2.8 billion

4.
UK
$2.7 billion

If you want to sell records, these are the countries to do it in!
≫ WORKBOOK 6

TIP

In the music industry, other countries are called 'territories'.
≫ WORKBOOK 7

RECORD LABELS

The key business in the recording industry is the record label. There are thousands of record labels throughout the UK, however, only five Major International companies at present: BMG, EMI, Sony, Warner and Universal. Each have a range of smaller labels, and they also license to and from independent labels to provide and cater for niche markets. Occasionally artists sign with smaller labels to remain independent and largely in control of their affairs, only to find that a major company has bought controlling shares in the label that they signed to.

There are many smaller independent record labels in the UK. These range in size from £ multi-million businesses to tiny one-man-band bedroom operations. Examples of successful indies include Beggars Group, XL and Ninja Tune. The indies are represented by a trade organisation called AIM (Association of Independent Music).

HOW DOES A RECORD COMPANY WORK?

ARTIST AND REPERTOIRE (A&R)

A&R department is responsible for finding, signing, recording and developing artists signed to the label. The A&R person is the initial point of record company contact for the manager. A&R departments receive hundreds of demos, read reviews, surf the web, watch dozens of acts live, and are contacted by numerous managers, agents and lawyers every week. Their job is to check out all of the above and predict the most successful candidates to fill gaps in the company's roster of artists. After the discovery they sign and develop this talent for the company, working closely with the act in its early stages and planning production and recording.

MARKETING

Marketing (also known as Product Management): this department is responsible for developing an image for the artist. Oversees video production, photo-sessions, artwork and media promotion.

BUSINESS AFFAIRS

Business Affairs department oversees and negotiates all contracts and agreements on behalf of the record company. Business Affairs staff are often lawyers and they will discuss, negotiate and agree terms of the record contract, recording budget, advance, and so on.

INTERNATIONAL

British talent accounts for a large proportion of international sales, and UK labels often have an international section which seeks to exploit their sound recordings in overseas markets.
This relies on an expert understanding of the different overseas legal systems.

PROMOTION

Promotion is responsible for all promotional activity. This area is usually sub-divided into press, TV / radio plugging, clubs and creative / video. Public perception and awareness often hinges on the media. The record company marketing team will plan a campaign to match release dates with television, radio, club reaction, newspaper and advertising coverage of a new product.

ADMINISTRATION

Various administrative roles include human resources (or personnel), legal / business affairs, finance and of course the Managing Director (MD) or Chief Executive Officer (CEO).

THE
MUSIC
PUBLISHING
INDUSTRY

The music publishing industry makes money by **exploiting the copyright in music that it owns**.
The key business is the **music publishing company**, which collects and creates revenue from the original songs and music written by its signed songwriters and composers.

≫ WORKBOOK 7 for more info on royalties, deals and contracts.

The key thing to remember about publishing is that money is collected and paid to the writers each time their music is played on the radio / TV or performed live in public. Money is also collected by publishers and paid to writers when print, synchronisation or Grand rights are licensed. Or (in classical publishing) when scores and parts are hired for performance purposes

For example, if you wrote a piece of music that was broadcast on BBC Radio One for 3 minutes, you would be entitled to a performance royalty of over £50. This royalty would be collected by the Performing Right Society (PRS) on your behalf and then distributed to you. (See P65 – collection societies).

HOW DOES A MUSIC PUBLISHING COMPANY WORK?

The job of the music publishing company is to exploit the rights in the original music written by its signed songwriters and composers. The company will sign up a writer and expect them to write music in return for (probably) an advance of money and a slice of the royalties generated by that music.
The songwriter is entitled to two royalties when working with a publishing company.

MECHANICAL ROYALTY (on any sound-carrier) – collected by **MCPS**
PERFORMING ROYALTY (live or broadcast) – collected by **PRS**

Money is also generated through print and synchronisation
For more information on MCPS and PRS see next section.

MUSIC PUBLISHING COMPANY

A&R ARTIST AND REPERTOIRE

is responsible for finding, signing and developing songwriters and composers signed to the publisher. They will try to attract record company A&R interest in order to have the songwriters' material recorded and released by their artists, or try and place the music with more established artists, thus generating PRS and MCPS royalties. In classical publishing, the equivalent of A&R is generally referred to as Promotion. People working in this sphere are forging links with festivals, orchestras and broadcasters with a view to securing commissions, performances and recordings.

ROYALTY TRACKING

administers royalties generated by the use of original music from writers and composers signed to the publishing company. Where original signed material is used for performance, broadcast or other commercial use, money is generated. A manager or accountant will normally check royalty statements on behalf of the songwriter.

BUSINESS AFFAIRS

oversees and negotiates all contracts and agreements on behalf of the publishing company.

Q. Are you clear with all that?

"**YES**, I completely understand how music publishing works"
There is always more to learn! Look at the weblinks and more tasks.

"**NO**, I still don't understand how music publishing works"
Don't worry! It takes time to understand this business. What is important to realise is that whenever you create an original piece of music, it has a value which can be exploited in the music marketplace. The publisher is the business that helps to exploit it for you. More later on this.

THE LIVE PERFORMANCE INDUSTRY

Consumers in the UK spend about £350 million a year on admission to concerts and gigs.
Playing and performing live is big business and creates jobs for many tens of thousands of people.

CABARET

Many musicians make a
good living by playing in
cabaret or function bands.
This can range from
small pubs and clubs to
quite large venues and
cruise ships or holiday
resorts abroad.

ORCHESTRAL

Orchestral musicians are
often on a full time wage
and make their living by
performing with an
orchestra in smaller
ensembles and
sometimes doing some
music teaching.
≫ WORKBOOK 9

TRIBUTE

There are 'tribute' bands
who play in the style of a
well known band, such as
Abba or the Beatles.

POP AND ROCK MUSIC

The biggest acts such as
The Rolling Stones and
Robbie Williams can
command huge fees for
playing live.
There is lots of work here
for roadies, session
musicians, techies, sound
engineers and many
others...

CLUBS

DJ's can play in venues ranging from local pubs to huge sellout arenas. Many DJ's work part time and have another job. Some operate professionally with their own equipment (this is called self-contained). In a big city with lots of students, like London, Manchester, Nottingham, Leeds or Glasgow, there is a lot of potential DJ work about. The superstar DJ's can command fees of £5000+ per night – but this is the exception rather than the norm.

KARAOKE

Karaoke presenters make a living from running karaoke nights in pubs and clubs. They are usually performers who can do a bit of singing and presenting. This is a big growth area.

SESSION / TOURING

Session musicians work as freelancers (self employed) for TV, radio, record labels, producers and recording studios. They often do some teaching to make up their salary, or even have a full time job as well. They sometimes get a lucrative contract to play in the 'pit band' in a musical, which involves months of regular work.
Touring session musicians work with the big touring pop acts and get very well paid when they are on tour, including daily expenses and all travel and accommodation.

CASE STUDIES

RECORDING INDUSTRY

INDEPENDENT RECORD LABEL MANAGER
– small UK specialist indie label

I manage a small label, putting out 10-15 releases a year. Everyday jobs are making telephone calls, completing label paperwork – clearances, agreements and similar and meeting with artists, managers and recording studios. I listen to all demos myself and keep in touch by DJ'ing myself.

You need to be interested in every aspect of the business and really know your music. I've never really been nervous of talking to people; being cheeky enough to ask gets you far.

I've been a graphic designer, a DJ in pubs and clubs, a promoter, done producing and remixing and then got involved with A&R for a local label. Now, I sort of use all those skills combined with a good sense of business to manage the label.

Good tips would be to believe in yourself, your own abilities and your judgement.
Your music may not be for everyone, but never let that bother you.

MUSIC PUBLISHING INDUSTRY

A&R MANAGER
– independent music publisher

The first thing you need is a total passion for music. You need to live, breathe and sleep music and know everything about what's happening musically.

I spend a lot of my day in an office environment, making calls, listening to music, talking to writers on our roster and dealing with labels, managers, publicists, designers and recording studios. My job is to find and develop writing talent that will hopefully make us all some money. The business is really competitive and it's really difficult to get into A&R unless you know people. So get to know them, and don't give up.

I also spend a lot of time going to gigs, showcases and recording studios in the evenings. It's the music industry so plenty of late nights and the occupational hazards that go with it, but don't expect to get a lie-in every morning.

You are dealing with creative people, so you need great people skills, as well as an excellent knowledge of music and commercial markets to channel the music into.

**LIVE
PERFORMANCE
INDUSTRY**

PROMOTER
– large UK promotions organisation, arranges tours
for international artists.

Working as a 'rep' for a large UK promotions
organisation, the job is to make sure everything
runs like clockwork, from the time that the bands
go out on tour – from changing budgets to liasing
with security, caterers, agents, sound and lighting
crews, to making sure that there are fresh towels in
the dressing room.

Top of the list of skills you need are 'people skills' –
knowing how to get results from people as well as
knowing how to calm them down.

Love your music, but don't be precious – it's a
business as well. Be prepared for hard work, late
nights and early mornings. I started out by working
in a pub, putting on local bands, then got in with a
national promoter. Best advice is to go to loads of
gigs and get to know the people who run these
things.

WHO ARE THE BUSINESS PEOPLE TO DEAL WITH?

Are you more interested in the business side of promoting and management?
≫ WORKBOOKS 6,7 and 8

AGENT

An agent is someone who gets work for the performer. In return, they take a commission – a percentage of your earnings. This is their payment for helping to get you the gig. There are music agents, concert agents, theatrical agents, DJ agencies... and so on. For large rock and pop gigs, the agent is responsible for booking all live appearances on behalf of the artist. The agent will normally be appointed by the manager. Commission is typically 15% of performance fee / ticket sales. An agent may work with many local promoters to set up a tour. DJ agencies will charge a commission of typically 15% of the performance fee.

VENUES

A venue can range from a corner in a local pub, to huge arenas. Every day in hundreds of towns and cities all over the UK, there are small gigs and performances happening in bars, pubs, restaurants, department stores, hotel lobbies and street corners. If you write songs that are performed in public places, you may be entitled to a PRS royalty.
≫ WORKBOOK 8 – CHAPTER 3

PROMOTER

The Promoter is responsible for co-ordinating all elements of individual live performances; sound and lighting equipment, tickets, posters and advertising. They take the ticket money and pay all the costs.
You will find a music promoter in every city and most towns in the UK. It's a tough job and promoters can (and often do) lose money.

You will find local promoters by speaking to the manager at local venues. You will national promoters by looking at the small print in adverts in papers and music magazines.

MERCHANDISE

This work may be franchised to a professional merchandiser but typically the work is undertaken by staff employed by the manager. Merchandised goods include T shirts, pens, mugs, stickers, posters, calendars and anything with the artist brand, name or likeness on it.

TOUR MANAGER

The Tour manager is responsible for the artist / musicians while the act is on tour. This includes hotels, transport, instruments, crew, punctuality and behaviour.

THE MEDIA

Workbook 6 explains how you can use the Media to promote your music. But what exactly is 'the Media' and why do you need to know about it? The parts of the media that are of interest to musicians, performers and DJ's are:

Radio:
National and local radio, pirate radio.
Television:
Terrestrial (BBC, ITV, Channel 4, five), Satellite and Cable (Sky).
Publishing:
Newspapers, magazines and specialist publications.

All these organisations can help you to promote your music, using articles, reviews, airplay and interviews. The media also forms part of the music industry, as radio and TV stations have to pay for the privilege of broadcasting music. (See p65 – collection societies)

INDUSTRY MEMBERSHIP ORGANISATIONS AND TRADE BODIES

There are a number of music industry organisations that represent the interests of writers, artists, publishers, musicians, managers, producers and record companies. Here are some of the best known organisations:

AIM
Association of Independent Music

AIM is a trade organisation which represents the interests of independent record labels.

British Academy of Composers & Songwriters

British Academy of Composers & Songwriters is a membership organisation for songwriters and composers.

BPI
British Phonographic Industry

The BPI is a trade organisation which represents the interests of UK record labels, particularly the majors.

British Music Rights

Promotes the interests of British composers, songwriters and publishers through lobbying, education, PR and events.

Equity

Equity is the union for actors and theatrical performers.

MIA
Music Industries Association

Represents the interests of UK businesses selling musical instruments and associated products.

MMF
Music Managers Forum

The MMF represents the interests of artist managers.

MPA
Music Publishers Association

MPA represents the interests of UK music publishers.

MPG
Music Producers Guild

MPG is a membership organisation which represents the interests of UK Music Producers.

MU
Musicians Union

The MU is a union that represents the interests of its musician members. New Deal customers get a reduced membership rate. Ask your MOLP!

These organisations do not guarantee any success for you in the music business but they can offer vital support in areas such as business, insurance, legal advice, contacts and career guidance. In some cases, you can join simply by paying a subscription, in others, you will have to fulfil certain professional criteria.

OTHER SERVICES PROVIDE ADDITIONAL SUPPORT TO THE MUSIC INDUSTRY.

For example: Education and training organisations (colleges, schools, universities, private training companies, teachers, lecturers, trainers, community musicians, music therapists), Music Industry associations such as Sound Sense, Regional Arts Boards, Local Authority Arts Officers, Music Education Council, Jazz Services.

COLLECTION SOCIETIES

The role of the collection societies will be fully explained in workbook 8 (Business and Money), but here is a summary.

WHAT DO COLLECTION SOCIETIES DO?

If you write, publish or play music that is performed, broadcast or commercially released in the form of a sound recording the following collection societies collect money (royalties) on your behalf:

PRS	**MCPS**	**PPL**	**PAMRA**
Performing Right Society	Mechanical Copyright Protection Society	Phonographic Performance limited	

The PRS collects a licence fee for the broadcast and public performance of music, on behalf of its members who are songwriters, composers and music publishers. This fee is distributed four times a year in the form of royalties to the copyright owner/s with a minimum of 50% always paid directly to the songwriter/s or composer/s.

>> WORKBOOK 8
– CHAPTER 3

The MCPS, on behalf of its members who are songwriters, composers and music publishers, collects a licence fee from record companies and any other business that embeds music in a sound bearing device (eg toys, computer games, greeting cards, films and TV programmes). This fee is distributed monthly in the form of royalties to the copyright owners. For any song / music that is published 100% of the royalty will be paid to the publisher.

PPL collects a royalty for the broadcast use and public performance of a recording. Part of the royalty is paid to the record company and part to the performers who appear on the recording. PPL is the record label's collection society.

>> WORKBOOK 8
– CHAPTER 3

PAMRA is the collection society for performers. If you have performed on a recording that has received airplay (on radio or TV), then you could be eligible for a royalty.

HOW DOES IT WORK IN PRACTICE?

Broadcasters such as the BBC have to pay PPL, PRS and MCPS for the broadcast use of recorded material and the music itself. The collection societies collect this money and distribute it to record companies, musicians, writers and publishers.

THE INTERNATIONAL MUSIC SCENE

Music is a global industry. The UK is a world leader in the writing and production of popular music.
It's quite possible to create music that you may never sell in your own country. Many musicians, writers and producers earn a good living from having their music released and performed overseas.

Examples:
The major record labels are all international, and have offices all over the world. If you sign to a record label in the UK, they can exploit your music in many other countries.

Even if you are signed up to an independent record label, they may have good connections with other European and international labels.

TRADE FAIRS

Small record labels, or freelance producers, remixers and songwriters don't have the resources to have offices all over the world.
Sometimes they do a deal with another record label, publisher or distributor in another country to sell their product.
Sometimes they do it themselves, by attending one of the numerous international music trade fairs that take place all over the world.

Examples:

MIDEM
Every January in Cannes (South of France)

SXSW (South by South West)
Every March in Texas, USA

Popkomm
Every August in Germany

These events are full of small labels, publishers, producers and writers trying to sell their products into a global marketplace that is hungry for music of all kinds and types.

It can cost quite a lot of money to attend these events. and there is no guarantee that you will find a customer for your music. Try to link up with a local music professional or organisation and see if they can take product out on your behalf. You can give them a cut if they generate some business for you.

INTERNET SEARCHING

INTRODUCTION

This brief guide will give you enough information to become a 'search' guru. Within the next 10 minutes you'll be fine-tuning your search skills to produce search results that are accurate and plentiful.

Generally, if you know a little about how something works you can operate it with greater skill. The same goes for the Internet, so we start off with a quick crash bang course on the Internet. Then we take a quick look at how the search engines actually work and how they rank the results from searches.

Then, straight to the tips and tricks of searching. Don't skip straight to this part as you won't be able to take full advantage of your new skills.

Finally, there is a brief list of search engines and browsers you can use to search the Internet.

THE SHORTEST EXPLANATION OF
HOW THE INTERNET WORKS
YOU'LL EVER FIND!

How does the Internet work? Well there's a long technical answer, a medium technical answer and a really short 'give me the facts' answer. We're going to go for the latter. Why, because it's all we need to know at this time and it can start getting messy!

Here we go.

A network is a collection of computers joined together usually by ethernet cables (a special type of cable like a telephone cable but with more wires).

It's also becoming common for networks to be wireless. This just means that special wireless transmitters and receivers are doing the job that the cable can do (just like a cordless phone). Computers at colleges and universities and offices are nearly always networked. When networked, computers can share files, print to one shared printer, share Internet connections and in some circumstances use software programs on other networked computers.

The Internet is basically a network on a global scale. Millions of computers and wires that are all connected together so they can share, store or converge information.

When you go on the Internet you are actually connecting 'to' the Internet to access, share or store information. From now on we'll call that information 'data' instead simply because data is a more generic term than information and can apply to lots of different things.

There are basically two types of computers on the Internet. These are Servers and clients.

SERVERS

Servers **serve** information (web servers) and clients **look** at information (e.g. Your computer at home/College/University/work etc).

So, think of the servers as being stacks of pc's (without the screen, keyboard and mouse) that live at Universities, large companies, Internet service providers (ISP's, like Wanadoo) and professional web hosting companies (companies that provide web server rental to web design agencies and other people that want to put websites on the Internet).

Generally, these servers are on 24hrs a day, 7 days a week (unless they crash and need to be restarted) serving information to clients all over the world through a variety of cables that carry the data.

So, there are literally millions of servers all over the world that store, share and converge all sorts of information. Servers are the hub of the Internet and without them the Internet would not function.

CLIENTS

Think of clients as being normal everyday computers connected to the Internet. So, once you connect a computer to the Internet it becomes a client and when you come offline (disconnect from the Internet) it is no longer a client.

LANGUAGE

They talk to each other using what are called 'protocols'. There are many different protocols, but the main one used for the Internet is called hypertext transfer protocol (or http- which is why web addresses start with http://).
To give you a better idea, another protocol is for sending email (smtp - simple mail transfer protocol) and another is for receiving email (pop - post office protocol - this is nothing to do with the post office, it's just its name). So, protocols allow different communication channels. This is a little confusing, but you don't need to understand this, you just need to know they all speak the same language.

So, now we know the language, how do they get the data from a server to a client? Well, the data (remember, information) is sent using a number of other protocols that are collectively called TCP/IP (transmission control protocol and Internet protocol). TCP/IP does the job of delivering the data to the correct address and makes sure all the data gets there in the right order.

So, let's say you go on the Internet and log onto
http://www.google.co.uk.
This is what happens.
First of all you connect to the Internet,

- using a dial up modem on a normal telephone line

or

- using a network connection at a place of work or some form of ISDN or broadband which are basically faster Internet connections.

Let's say you are using a dial up connection from home, the number you dial (on the PC) connects you to your ISP (Internet service provider). You are then on the Internet. You open up your browser (the program that lets you see Internet pages, like Microsoft's Internet Explorer) and type in the address http://www.google.co.uk and hit enter.
Kappooow. Your request is sent down the wire to the ISP web servers which automatically redirect the data to Google's servers. Then the Google servers send you back the data you requested via the quickest route.

The data quite often travels around the world at least once before you receive the page!

In a nutshell, that's about it!

HOW DO THE SEARCH ENGINES WORK AND HOW DO THEY RANK THEIR RESULTS?

There are 3 types of search engines.

CRAWLER-BASED SEARCH ENGINES

They're called crawler-based because a little program called a search robot (sometimes called spider or agent) 'crawls' the web looking at websites and gathering information. Think of them as reading the content of the website. They also look at specific data that can be inputted by the web designer when the site is built.

This information is called meta data and is supposed to give the search robot a clear idea of the most important words. phrases and information on that site. This information allows the search engine to create a directory of websites that can be searched. This process is virtually fully automated. These little 'robots' are constantly crawling the web looking at websites and placing information about them into a large database.

SEARCH DIRECTORIES

These are directories made by people (not automated like crawler-based engines). Website administrators send a brief description of their website to the search directory and eventually someone working with or for the search directory will rank the site according to its suitability for a category.

It can take months to rank a site on a search directory.

COMBINATION

Generally most search engines use both human developed directories and crawler-based directories.

HOW DO THE SEARCH ENGINES RANK THEIR RESULTS?

When you perform a search the search engine has to go through billions of pages to find the most relevant results. The search engine looks at various aspects of the websites to decide how to rank each site. Different search engines generally return different results because they look at different aspects of a website and therefore come up with a slightly different results. Each search engine uses a complex mathematical equation (called an algorithm) to determine how to rank each website.

Because search engine ranking is such a competitive industry in itself, no-one really knows exactly what search engines are looking for but there is a general consensus that the following factors are extremely important to achieve a good ranking with a search engine.

LOCATION AND FREQUENCY

If the words 'music' and 'producer' appear in a website title or domain name, but the word is only listed a few times on the actual website and these words are towards the bottom of a page, then that site will not be ranked highly by the search engine.
However, if the website had a domain of www.themusicproducer.com and the title of one of the pages was 'the music producer' and the first line of every paragraph in this page started with 'The music producer', then the site would have a better chance of receiving a good ranking.

YOU CAN'T KID ME!

If a website has the same word repeated over and over again the search engine robot will think the website developer is trying to cheat their way to a higher ranking than deserved, so the robot will either ban the website from being listed, or simply ignore the website and move on.

LINKS

Search robots look at how many links there are to and from page and calculate how popular each page probably is. This again determines the rank of each website.

TRAFFIC

The more traffic a website receives, the higher the ranking and vice versa.

MONEY TALKS!

So, the problem is the search engines are rewarding web developers who know how to create pages to receive high rankings. That's no good to most small businesses who cannot afford or do not want the expense of employing a 'search engine optimisation' expert to design their website for better ranking. This puts more emphasis on our ability to conduct accurate searches.

TIPS AND TRICKS

"Getting information from the Internet is like getting a glass of water from Niagara Falls"
Arthur C Clarke (2000)

The most important aspect of improving your searching skills is practice. Get as much practice as possible with the various techniques listed below. Only with practice will you become an expert.

WHICH SEARCH ENGINE SHOULD I USE?

First, a decision needs to be made on which search engine to use. At this moment, Google is the most accurate and most widely used. However, if you are not getting the results you are looking for with Google, you could always try another search engine (see the list at the end of this section). Google has a number of ways you can search including the default web search or directory, groups and news listings searches. The directory is very useful and many searchers now use this before trying the web search. The directory search enables you to dig deeper and deeper into a specific topic and is best for broad ranging searches. It can be a little more time consuming than a web search.

WHAT AM I LOOKING FOR?

The phrase you type into the search box has to be an accurate summary of what you are looking for. Before you type anything in, have a quick think about what you are looking for and if possible write out the question that you need answering or something about the topic you are researching. Then pick out the most common words and put them together (in a phrase if possible). Always use lower case letters, as this will ensure your search returns both upper and lower case (this doesn't matter with Google). Remember some words are spelt differently in American English so you may need to compensate for this. Some words are commonly misspelt so you could try the various spellings within your search. You can also try using singular and plural phrases (e.g. music producers and music producer). Strangely, the order in which your search phrase appears will also make a difference (e.g. Music producer will produce a different result than producer music). If you are looking for something specifically in the UK, try the www.google.co.uk search or try inputting UK at the end of your search.
Be as specific as possible. Asking questions sometimes works well.

FINE TUNING YOUR SEARCH

This sounds much more complex than it is.
Including either a plus + minus - or speech marks " " in your search will enable you to really fine tune what you are looking for.

```
+
```

Using this ensures your search returns pages with all the words in your search phrase.

```
+music +producer
```

This will return results with both words on the same page. There is no limit on the number of words you use but generally search engines only allow for the first 10 words.

```
-
```

Using the minus function ensures your search returns pages with the word after the - omitted
For example, let's say you wanted to find information on music producers, but not engineers

```
+music +producer -engineers
```

```
" "
```

Placing your phrase or words within speech marks ensures the words are next to each other on the web page

Let's say we wanted to fine tune our search even more and find pages with the words music producer together but not with the words engineer or manager

```
"music producers" -engineers -manager
```

Now to fine tune even more, let's say we are looking for music producers with their own studio

```
"music producers" -engineers -manager +studio +owner
```

EVEN MORE FINE TUNING!

BASIC INFORMATION ABOUT BOOLEAN SEARCHING

This is the use of boolean operators for searching. The 2 most common are AND and OR. Google by default uses AND. So if, you search for 'music producers' Google will automatically look for pages with both words. If you use the OR operator then the search will be for either the word music or producer within a web page. If you prefer you can use the pipe character (|) instead of the OR word.

```
"music producers" -engineers -manager +studio OR owner
```

This search phrase will look for web pages with the words music and producer together without the words engineer or manager and with the word studio or owner.

SPECIAL SYNTAX

intext:
This will enable you to search just the text. It's really handy for searching the actual website content rather than the information the website administrator has placed to improve the ranking of the site.
For example,

```
intext:"music producers" +studio OR owner
```

related:
Related allows you to look for websites related to the URL(website address) in the search

```
related:www.google.com
```

This will return websites that are in some way related to Google.

* WILDCARDS

A wild card can be any word. This comes in useful when you are not sure of a word or phrase. * = any word

```
"red sky at night is a * delight"
```

This will return both 'sailor' and 'shepherd' answers.

ADVANCED SEARCHING WITH GOOGLE

Google has its very own advanced search function. This enables you to be really specific about what you are for. It's easy to operate as you just need to complete the form on the advanced search page. The advanced is self-explanatory but takes some practice to get used to.

SEARCH ENGINE LIST

BROWSER LIST

This is a recommended list of search engines. Try to get used to using two or three and becoming accustomed to the type of results they return. You'll quickly find that some are better than others for certain searches

Some browsers can return results quicker than others. Try experimenting with the following:

PC
Internet Explorer
Opera
Netscape
Mozilla

MAC
Safari
Opera
Internet Explorer

www.google.co.uk

www.alltheweb.com

www.yahoo.com

www.hotbot.com

www.lycos.com

www.teoma.com

WANT TO KNOW MORE?

LINKS

New Deal for Musicians has no responsibility for or control of the following sites. The inclusion of any site does not necessarily imply New Deal for Musicians approval of the site. To access any of the sites please type in the address into a browser or search using keywords from the name of the link. www.dfes.gov.uk/ukonlinecentres Find Internet access that's close to you.

INFORMATION AND LINKS ABOUT THE MUSIC INDUSTRY

- [ ] www.musictank.co.uk/training_res.htm
  First class source of information on the music industry, including news.

- [ ] www.bmr.org/html/guide2.html
  On-line guide to how the industry works for writers and writer-performers

- [ ] www.mcps-prs-alliance.co.uk
  A full explanation of how PRS and MCPS work. You can also download a map of how the music industry works. (Search for Music Universe)

- [ ] www.mi2n.com
  Music Industry News Network. Keep up to date with news and whats going on

- [ ] www.musicweek.co.uk
  The music industry trade paper

- [ ] www.bbc.co.uk/radio1/onemusic/howto/
  Over 80 in depth guides taking you from starting to make music to getting it heard.

TRADE FAIRS

- [ ] www.midem.com
  Midem International Music Market, Cannes Huge annual conference in Cannes, France. Major European and USA delegation.

- [ ] www.sxsw.com
  South by South West
  Annual conference in Austin, Texas: loads of indie/rock.alternative/electronic bands : lots of industry types.

- [ ] www.wmcon.com
  Winter Music Conference
  Annual conference in Miami - dance and electronic based.

- [ ] www.cmj.com
  Huge annual conference in New York, loads of indie/rock.alternative/electronic bands and college radio stations. CMJ The Magazine focuses on college radio and touring bands on the college circuit.

- [ ] www.inthecity.co.uk
  In The City International Music Convention, Manchester

- [ ] www.popkomm.de
  International music exhibition and trade fair in Germany

- [ ] www.musicworksuk.com
  MusicWorks New Music Convention & Festival, Glasgow International Cross-Media Music Convention. State of the Nation Showcasing new music by young and emerging composers.

INDUSTRY AND TRADE ORGANISATIONS

☐ www.musicindie.org
AIM (The Association of Independent Music)
British Association of Independent record
companies and distributors

☐ www.aprs.co.uk
APRS (Association of Professional Recording
Services)
The APRS promotes standards of
professionalism and quality within the audio
industry.

☐ www.aurauk.com
AURA (Association of United Recording Artists)
Membership association representing the
interests of professional recording artists. AURA
primarily looks after the interests of featured
artists and studio producers, membership is
exclusive to performers and studio producers
who have performed on a commercially released
recording

☐ www.britishacademy.com
The British Academy of Composers and
Songwriters is the largest composer/songwriter
membership organisation in the world,
representing the interests of over 3,000 UK
music writers. Good info on song competitions
and classical composition competitions etc, plus
some good links.

☐ www.bmr.org
BMR (British Music Rights)
Promoting the rights of British music
composers, songwriters and publishers.
Includes an interactive guide to the music
business and how it works, with links to other
organisations and descriptions of who's who.

☐ www.bmr.org/html/acronyms.html
A good list of organisations and acronyms with
links

☐ www.bpi.co.uk
BPI (British Phonographic Industry)
The British Phonographic Industry (BPI)
represents the interests of British record
companies and organises the BRIT awards.
Good site, for professionals but does have a DIY
guide to creating your own record label and
some other industry advice. Access all areas
leaflet is £3.50 on the site

☐ www.ism.org
ISM (Incorporated Society of Musicians)
A professional body for musicians, the site has
useful information on careers, rates of pay and
lists of members who are teachers. Particularly
useful for classical musicians and teachers.

☐ www.makingmusic.org.uk
Making Music
(formerly the National Federation of Music
Societies)
Represents over 2000 amateur music groups,
such as choirs, orchestras and music promoters.
Various services and information available.

INDUSTRY AND TRADE ORGANISATIONS

www.ukmmf.net
MMF (Music Managers Forum)
The MMF (Music Managers Forum) represents the interests of Managers in the music industry and provides comprehensive training.

www.mpaonline.org.uk
MPA (Music Publishers Association)
Representing the interests of music publishers to the Government, music industry, media and public. Offers a jobseekers service, lists of publishers and information on careers.

www.mpg.org.uk
MPG (The Music Producers Guild Ltd)
The Music Producers Guild promotes and represents all individuals in the music production and recording professions.

www.musiciansunion.org.uk
MU (Musician's Union)
Trade union representing interests of musicians. Contains very useful information, tip sheets etc. for working musicians, for example on contracts, health and safety and gigging.

www.pamra.org.uk
PAMRA (Performing Artists Media Rights Association) A non-profit making organisation run by performers for performers, PAMRA administers the broadcasting royalties for and represents the interests of over 16,000 artists.

www.pact.co.uk
PACT (The Producers Alliance for Cinema and Television)
The trade association in the UK representing independent television, film, animation and new media production companies. Training and publications available.

www.pcam.co.uk
PCAM (Society for Producers and Composers of Applied Music)
The UK trade association for producers and composers who work primarily in commissioned music for advertising, television programmes and feature films. List of members according to their type of work.

www.ppluk.com
PPL (Phonographic Performance Ltd) PPL is a music industry collecting society representing over 3,000 record companies, from the large multinationals to the small independents.It also licenses recordings to broadcasting organisations and to public performance venues which use recorded music, such as pubs and shops.

www.mcps-prs-alliance.co.uk
Website for PRS and MCPS

www.musicmall.co.uk
Video Performance Ltd - a collection society set up by the record industry to grant licences to users of music videos.

BOOKS AND MAGAZINES

☐ **All You Need To Know About The Music Industry**
Passman, Donald
Publisher : Simon and Schuster, Inc.
ISBN : 0743246373

☐ **How to make it in the Music Business**
Pattenden, Sian
Publisher : Virgin Books
ISBN : 0753504219

☐ **Music Week – Music Week Directory 2004**
Publisher : CMP Information
ISBN : 0863825532

☐ **The Guerilla Guide to the Music Business**
Sarah Davis, David Laing
Publisher : Continuum International Publishing
Group - Academi
ISBN : 0826447007

MORE TASKS

1 Do more research on your favourite artists, producers or DJ's. Once you have found out the record label and publisher, search for management and other professional business advisers. Develop a database of contacts for you to market your product to.

2 If you want to go into business as a label, producer, manager or publisher, do more research about joining the relevant trade associations (e.g. AIM, MMF or MPG). Are you eligible to join? – get hold of the application forms and read them, speak to your MIC or MOLP.

3 Do you have some musical product that you think could sell overseas? If so, do more research on international trade fairs such as MIDEM and SXSW. Find someone else who is going – and provide them with some product to market. If you want to attend yourself, prepare a costing and work with your MOLP to try and identify funding.

4 Name three benefits to being part of a trade organisation.
   1)
   2)
   3)

5 Find and read a copy of Music Week
   - write 3 new things you have found out
   1)
   2)
   3)

6 Find out more about the value of the UK recording industry.
   - of the £3billion spent buying recorded music, which type of genre of music sells the most?
   - which age group of the public spends the most money buying music?

photography Ray Chan

TO DO LIST

1. Wash hands in warm water before practice
2. Loosen fingers, stretching fingers and shaking hands
3. 2 mins play chromatic scale in F over three octaves, ascending and descending in quavers at 70 BPM
4. 30 secs break — WALK THE DOG
5. 1 min C major scale ascending and descending in quavers at 70 BPM CONSISTENTLY WITHOUT STOPPING
6. 20 secs break
7. 1 min C Major scale — 75 BPM
8. Clean myself up
9. Phone mother
10. 1 min C Major scale — 70 BPM
11. 10 mins work on "Hey Joe" by Jimi Hendrix, using these chords ...ssion Watch Eastenders

Setting Your Goals

WHAT IS IT?

We all need to know what our goals are – how else will we get there?

Setting goals, making action plans and keeping track of how you're doing, are important parts of the MOLP programme.

You need to:

- think carefully about what drives you, what you're good at and let this help you plan what goals to set

- make a fair judgement about what your skills and experience are at the moment

- identify anything which is stopping you from moving forward

- plan realistic goals, which you can achieve within a reasonable time

WHY DO I NEED TO KNOW ABOUT THIS?

Setting unrealistic goals usually ends in lack of confidence and motivation – you need to prove to yourself that you can do things, not set yourself up for goals which are too far away as yet.

Setting realistic, achievable goals which you CAN reach in a reasonable time, will encourage, inspire and motivate you to carry on down your chosen path.

Big bridges are made from little bricks.

These are skills which will HELP you throughout your life.

Now ask two other people to do the same exercise.
They should be people you respect, who can give an honest opinion of you. For instance, a fellow band member or a close friend.

		person 1	person 2
HOW DO YOU RATE YOUR PERSONAL SKILLS?			
1	**How good are you at organising and planning?** - are you often late; do you keep a diary; do you have a daily 'job' list?	/10	/10
2	**How good are you at solving problems?** - do you panic when things go wrong; can you plan your way out of problems; do others turn to you to help them with problems?	/10	/10
3	**How good are you at communicating in writing?** - can you easily write notes; letters; application forms?	/10	/10
4	**How good are you at communicating by speaking, including on the telephone?** - can you easily speak to people you don't know; do you get the right answer when you ask questions; do you know what to say and how to say it when you're on the telephone?	/10	/10
5	**How good are you at working with others?** - can you accept direction, ideas and constructive criticism; do you find it easy to work with other musicians; does your temper flare when you don't agree with what others say?	/10	/10
6	**How good are you at using numbers?** - can you plan a budget for a gig; can you work out how much your demo will cost you; can you work out how many door staff you need for an event for children based on a ratio of 1:25?	/10	/10
7	**How good are your IT skills?** - are you able to easily use a computer to word process; to save and print documents; to access the Internet?	/10	/10
8	**How good are you at thinking and working creatively?** - are you an 'ideas' person; do you find it easy to write songs or music; do you concentrate on the practical issues in life, or on the creative side of your life?	/10	/10
HOW DO YOU FEEL ABOUT YOURSELF?			
9	Motivation	/10	/10
10	Confidence	/10	/10
11	Health – physical and mental	/10	/10
HOW DO YOU RATE YOUR MUSICAL SKILLS AND TALENT?			
12	Performing ability as a musician / performer / DJ	/10	/10
13	Musical Knowledge	/10	/10
14	Music Business knowledge	/10	/10
15	Creative Talent (writing and arranging)	/10	/10
16	Business sense and judgement	/10	/10

If you recognise your weaker points, you can do something about them!

This is only a small list of the skills you will have.
Also read workbook 2 chapter 2 Skills and Experience.

Now compare the results of this exercise with your own assessment. Are the results similar or different?

Are the results **SIMILAR**? → You have a clear perception of your strengths and weaknesses and the skills you will have.

Are the results **DIFFERENT**? → You may not be fully aware of your strengths and weaknesses

4 SETTING YOUR GOALS AND ACTION PLANS

You should now work out some long term and short term career and personal goals and decide how to make them happen.

≫ Your professional goals are dealt with in more detail in WORKBOOK 2 – CHAPTER 2.

Look at the sample 'CAREER GOAL' and 'PERSONAL GOAL' action plans on P104-105.

Create your own action plan.

CAREER GOAL ACTION PLAN

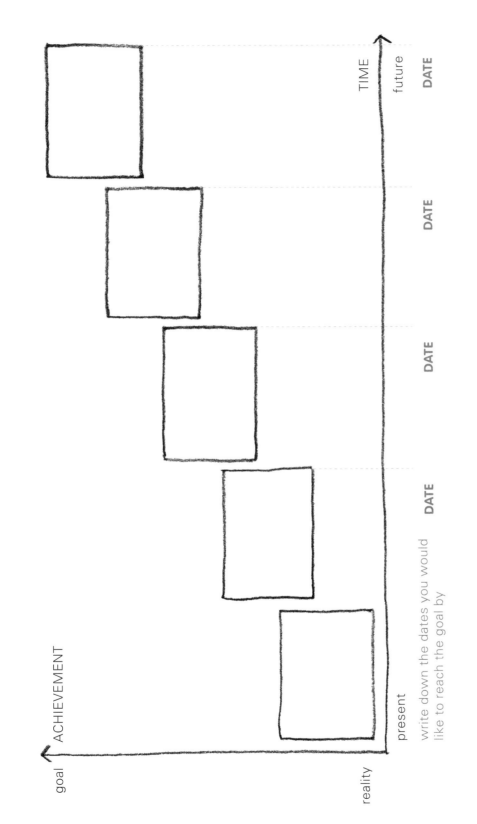

goal ← ACHIEVEMENT

reality

present

write down the dates you would
like to reach the goal by

DATE   DATE   DATE   DATE   DATE

TIME

future

PERSONAL GOAL ACTION PLAN

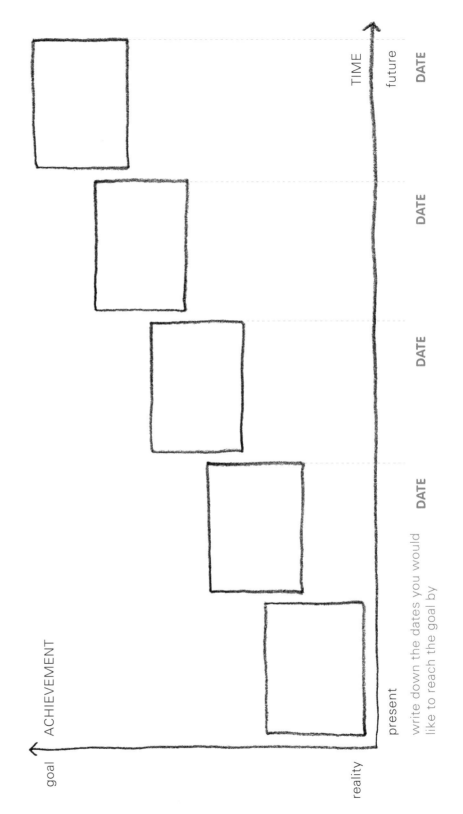

goal ← ACHIEVEMENT

reality

present

write down the dates you would
like to reach the goal by

DATE   DATE   DATE   DATE   DATE

TIME

future

WELL DONE, THAT'S THE END OF THIS ASSIGNMENT. CHECK IT AND HAND IT IN!

WHAT do I do now?
Read the TASKS section below.
Then read the NOTES AND GUIDANCE section.
Carry out the TASKS.

HOW will I be assessed?
Your tutor will assess your work. He / she will give you feedback on how you have done. If your work needs further work to be passed, then you will be given the chance to do further work to bring it "up to scratch". For more details, please refer to your MOLP's own guidance.

HOW LONG should this assignment take?
Every person works at his / her own pace. As a guide, this should take you 5 hours to read and research and another 2 hours to write your answers and discuss them with your tutor.

TIP
You will come back to your answers to this project during your time on MOLP, to see how you are progressing – be as honest in your answers as possible!

1 YOUR PERSONALITY

Read the notes on Your Personality in notes and guidance P95. Think about your interests, what you enjoy the most and are naturally good at.

Which 'personality type' best describes you? (tick one or more)

☐ You are interested in science and how or why things work.

You may be interested in music technology, or a research and development role.

☐ You like to be around people and to help them.

If you are at ease with others, your personality might be leading you towards artist management or promoting your own music. If you're good at helping others, have you thought about teaching?

☐ You like to be in charge and are a good communicator.

You have an interest in the organisation and management of things. You might be good at setting up your own business as a singer or writer, or helping others to do the same.

☐ You like reading and writing and have an ability to express yourself in words.

Music journalism is a great opportunity, but you might also put yourself forward as the band member who writes the press releases.

☐ You enjoy artistic things like art, drama, music and dance.

You're probably the creative one, experimenting with different ideas or getting a kick out of producing or re-mixing.

☐ You enjoy working with numbers and have a keen interest in computers.

Rather than just liking computers, you enjoy working with numbers and calculating things but also have a keen interest in learning more about computers and programming. Producing or marketing your music on the Internet might be right up your street.

☐ You like seeing how things work and fixing them.

Engineering is your thing! You will be good at maintaining and repairing equipment and possibly one for detail on the settings of your gear. Technical and roadie work is right up your street.

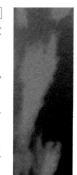

☐ You prefer to be outdoors.

You are an "outdoor" person, preferring to be outdoors wherever possible no matter what the weather. You might be interested in being a community musician, spreading the work that you do in a wider field, or want to look at tour related or festival work.

TIP
Remember this, when you come to read workbook 2 – work and jobs. Plan your career around what you're good at and you are likely to succeed!

Read the notes and guidance on P96, then answer the following questions, giving yourself marks out of 10. Be honest and realistic!

MARK **✱** wherever you need to improve that skill.

			marks / 10	✱ mark here
HOW DO YOU RATE YOUR PERSONAL SKILLS?	1	**How good are you at organising and planning?** – are you often late; do you keep a diary; do you have a daily 'job' list?	/ 10	
	2	**How good are you at solving problems?** – do you panic when things go wrong; can you plan your way out of problems, do others turn to you to help them with problems?	/ 10	
	3	**How good are you at communicating in writing?** – can you easily write notes; letters; application forms?	/ 10	
	4	**How good are you at communicating by speaking, including on the telephone?** – can you easily speak to people you don't know; do you get the right answer when you ask questions; do you know what to say and how to say it when you're on the telephone?	/ 10	
	5	**How good are you at working with others?** – can you accept direction, ideas and constructive criticism; do you find it easy to work with other musicians; does your temper flare when you don't agree with what others say?	/ 10	
	6	**How good are you at using numbers?** – can you plan a budget for a gig; can you work out how much your demo will cost you; can you work out how many door staff you need for an event for children based on a ratio of 1:25?	/ 10	
	7	**How good are your IT skills?** – are you able to easily use a computer to word process; to save and print documents; to access the Internet?	/ 10	
	8	**How good are you at thinking and working creatively?** – are you an 'ideas' person; do you find it easy to write songs or music; do you concentrate on the practical issues in life, or on the creative side of your life?	/ 10	
HOW DO YOU FEEL ABOUT YOURSELF? If you recognise your weaker points, you can do something about them!	9	Motivation	/ 10	
	10	Confidence	/ 10	
	11	Health – physical and mental	/ 10	
HOW DO YOU RATE YOUR MUSICAL SKILLS AND TALENT? This is only a small list of the skills you will have. Also read workbook 2 chapter 2 Skills and Experience.	12	Performing ability as a musician / performer / DJ	/ 10	
	13	Musical Knowledge	/ 10	
	14	Music Business knowledge	/ 10	
	15	Creative Talent (writing and arranging)	/ 10	
	16	Business sense and judgement	/ 10	

Your
Personality

Of course, you already know your personality, but it's easy to forget about what we are naturally good at when we're planning for the future. We seldom focus on ourselves and give ourselves time to think about the type of activities that come naturally to us.

TIP

Jobsearch staff, careers advisers and others may have access to more detailed personality profile programmes. Personality profiling is a commonly used system in applying for many jobs these days.

photography Ray Chan

Your Personal Skills

In whatever career you end up in, employers are going to look to you to prove that you have personal skills which are skills which you can take to all sorts of jobs and levels.
Examples of these skills are:

- team working
- IT skills
- problem solving skills
- communication skills
- planning skills

Although you want to focus on your career in music, you will stand a better chance of getting work if you are good at the OTHER things, as well as your musical abilities!

 TIP

None of this means that you are "selling out" your creativity. Instead, it means that you are giving yourself the real chance to make a viable living from your creative work, make your mark and make a difference. The world is full of musicians who say "I could have ....." but never did.

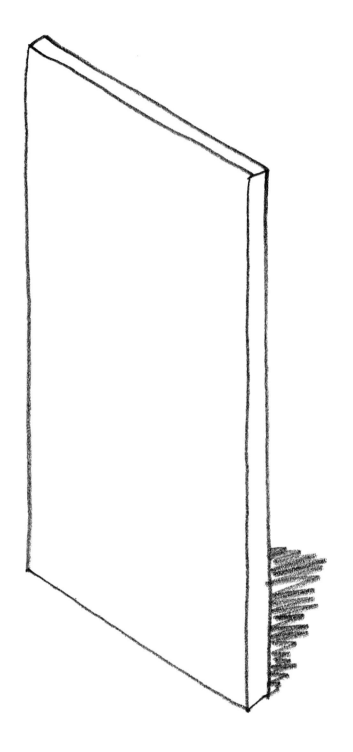

What's Stopping You?

If you've set yourself goals before, which you haven't achieved, give yourself a moment to think about why this might be.
Common reasons are:

- time
- money
- the right people to help you
- motivation
- personal circumstances—relationships, housing, health, responsibilities for other people, alcohol, drugs, criminal record
- health, disability
- skills, training or experience including basic skills
- confidence

If you can identify what's getting in your way, you can do something about it. Talk to your tutor, your MIC or your New Deal Adviser about these things – there might be something that they can do to help!

Musical
Skills
And
Talent

Fill in this questionnaire

QUESTION	ANSWER
How would you rate your level of playing or performance skills?	
What is the largest audience you have played or performed in front of?	
Have you ever been paid for playing, performing or writing music?	
How many other musicians do you know?	
How many other music industry people do you know? (manager, promoter, agent, lawyer etc)	
Have you dealt professionally with a manager, agent or lawyer?	
Can you read or write music?	
Have you got any qualifications in music or related areas?	

It is often easy to look back over a period of time and think that you have achieved nothing.
In fact, you may well have made good progress. It often takes 3 to 5 years, or even longer, before most people are able to make a viable living from music. As time passes by, you naturally learn more. It is important to note this and to compare your original ideas with the ones you have now.

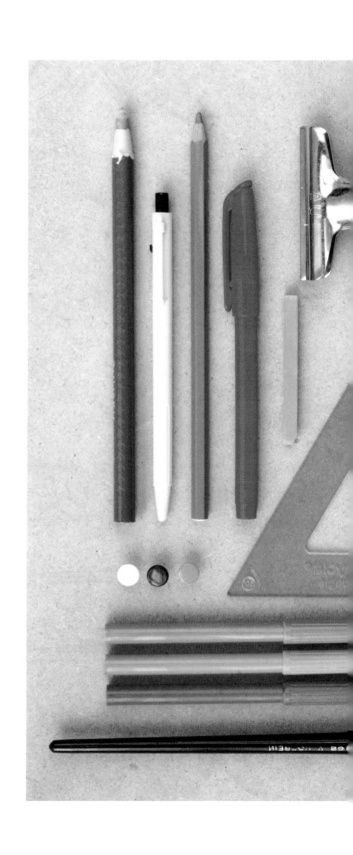

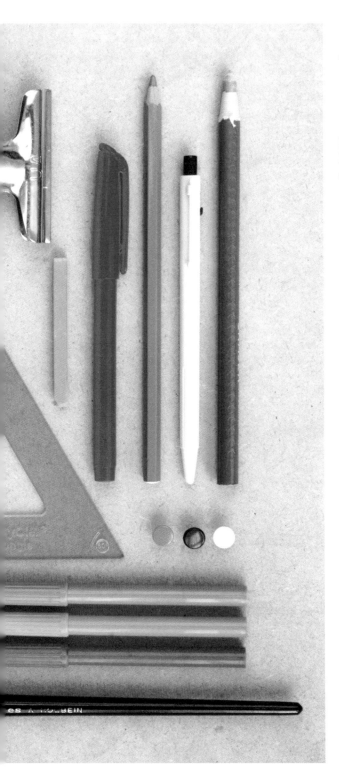

Action Planning

Planning is the key to success!
Here are some examples of things you need to have an action plan for.

ACTION PLAN TO MAKE THINGS HAPPEN

Playing first live gig to an audience

Getting paid for a live gig

Playing with more than one other group or ensemble live

Meeting or dealing with a music agent or manager

Meeting a music lawyer

Reading a contract

Playing in a recording studio

ACTION PLAN TO AVOID MISTAKES AND PROBLEMS

Electrical power cutting off on gig

Agent or promoter not paying fee

Argument with security staff

Argument over soundcheck time

Having no money to pay a hotel bill

Forgetting key piece of equipment

Leaving a printing job for flyers too late

Tripping over cables and damaging ankle

Creating Your Action Plan

Career Goal Plan

The first rule is: Split the job up into smaller chunks that you can achieve. Let's look at an example of a CAREER GOAL. See how Jim breaks down his goal into 'building blocks' and then sets realistic dates when he can do them by.

1
Jim is a bedroom DJ who plays trance and techno.

2
He has played at a few parties, but never got paid yet.

3
His ultimate goal is to get a residency at a club.

4
So how will he get there?

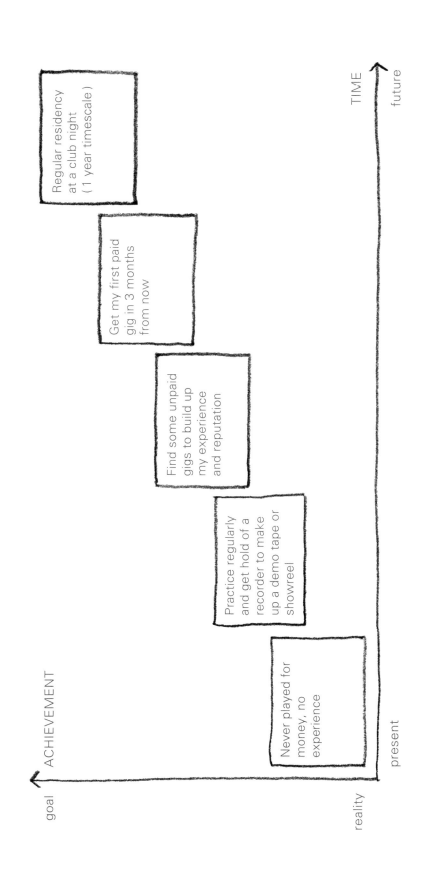

goal

ACHIEVEMENT

Regular residency at a club night (1 year timescale)

Get my first paid gig in 3 months from now

Find some unpaid gigs to build up my experience and reputation

Practice regularly and get hold of a recorder to make up a demo tape or showreel

Never played for money, no experience

reality

present

TIME

future

Personal Goal Plan

The first rule is: Split the job up into smaller chunks that you can achieve. Let's look at an example of a PERSONAL GOAL

1

Emma is a vocalist and lyric writer.

2

She wants to have the confidence to talk to people who she doesn't know and to share her ideas with groups of people.

3

Her goal is to get to know some other musicians so she can perform at acoustic nights and jam sessions.

4

So how will she get there?

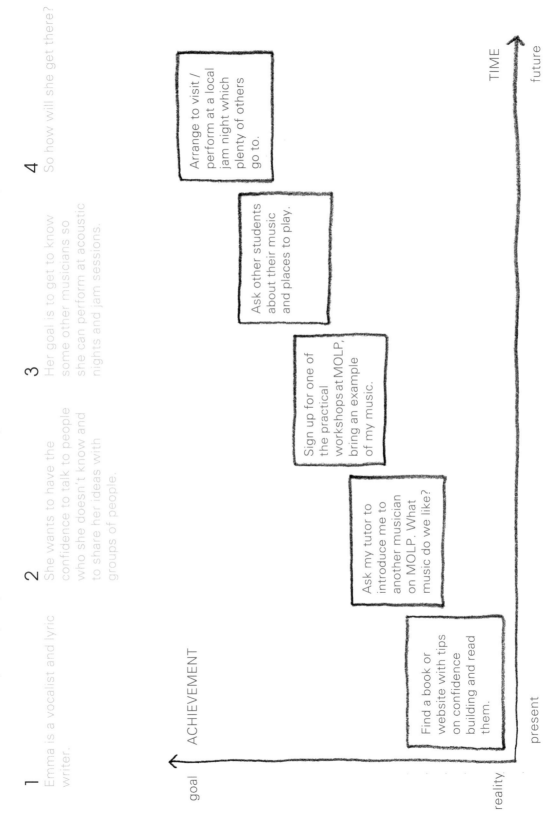

goal

ACHIEVEMENT

Find a book or website with tips on confidence building and read them.

Ask my tutor to introduce me to another musician on MOLP. What music do we like?

Sign up for one of the practical workshops at MOLP, bring an example of my music.

Ask other students about their music and places to play.

Arrange to visit / perform at a local jam night which plenty of others go to.

reality

present

TIME

future

Deciding
What's
Important

Its amazing how many people let opportunities slip past them, simply because they fail to understand when an opportunity comes their way. Learn to recognise an opportunity and when to seize it.

Here are two examples of situations that a musician might find themselves in. See if you think they are an opportunity or not.

Exercise 1.

You meet someone at your gig who says they are a manager, and they reel off loads of big names they have worked with. They want to get you into the studio as soon possible to record some tracks, and can virtually guarantee a record deal now that they have heard your material.

A few days later, the manager rings you again, emphasising the fact that he is excited about your songs. He knows a local studio who will do a cut price recording session, it will only cost you about £150.

What do you do?

Answer to exercise 1

Tread carefully. He could be genuine, but why isn't he putting his money where his mouth is? If he is an established manager with a track record, then finding studio time cheaply or even for nothing should not be a problem. He seems to be a little too pushy to get you into the studio without finding out more about you first.

Exercise 2.

You are playing with a pop band who are looking for a deal, but need to supplement your miserly income with some paid session work. A musician friend of yours rings you up and tells you that she has recommended you for the guitarist's job on a forthcoming European tour with a band who were quite well known a few years back. Its good money and the tour starts next week, but it's for 3 months and there are some (unpaid) gigs coming up with your own band.
What do you do?

Answer to exercise 2

It depends on your short term and long term aims. Examine your motivations - will doing the European tour help to satisfy your own career aims - maybe it will get you more and better paid work, and the chance to work with top class musicians? Or are you totally committed to your band? Can you compromise for three months? These type of decisions are part and parcel of being in music. Only you can decide, but it is certainly an opportunity!

WANT TO KNOW MORE?

LINKS

New Deal for Musicians has no responsibility for or control of the following sites. The inclusion of any site does not necessarily imply New Deal for Musicians approval of the site. To access any of the sites please type in the address into a browser or search using keywords from the name of the link. www.dfes.gov.uk/ukonlinecentres Find Internet access that's close to you.

PERSONAL DEVELOPMENT AND SUPPORT

☐ **www.bbc.co.uk/radio1/onelife**
look in the 'work' and 'interviews' sections for information about personality and interests tests. The site also has sections about housing, money, relationships – check it out.

☐ **www.support4learning.co.uk**
lots of links to sites with information on skills, interests, personality profiles, action planning and finance.

☐ **www.samaritans.org.uk**
24 hour a day support line, you can talk to a real person in confidence about anything which is troubling you - 08457 90 90 90 for the price of a local call.

☐ **www.shelter.org.uk**
The UK's national housing charity. Online advice about housing and a freephone number for confidential support - 0808 800 4444

☐ **www.bbc.co.uk/health**
Deals with a range of health issues, including physical and mental health, confidence, relationships and stress.

☐ **www.dwp.gov.uk**
Government site of the 'Department for Work and Pensions', which links to the Jobcentre Plus website dealing with all aspects of benefits and looking for work.

☐ **www.adviceguide.org.uk**
Citizens Advice website with advice on a full rage of issues, from benefits to housing, debts and legal rights.

BOOKS AND MAGAZINES

☐ **Personal effectiveness**
Alex Murdock and Carol N. Scutt. - 3rd ed.
Publisher : Butterworth-Heinemann, 2003
(Chartered Management Institute series).
ISBN : 0750656220

☐ **Secrets of performing confidence : for actors, musicians, performers, presenters**
Evans, Andrew.
Publisher : A. & C. Black, 2003.
ISBN : 0713662883

☐ **Successful interview skills : how to present yourself with confidence**
Corfield, Rebecca. - 3rd ed.
Publisher : Kogan Page, 2002.
ISBN : 0749438924

☐ **Improving your spelling : boost your word power and your confidence**
Field, Marion.
Publisher : How To Books, 2000.
(How To series)
ISBN : 1857035631

☐ **Returning to work : a guide to re-entering the job market**
Longson, Sally. - 2nd ed.
Publisher : How To Books, 2002
ISBN : 1857037863

MORE TASKS

1 Find 3 weblinks or books which contain tests in the following:
   - personality profiling
   - psychometric tests

   Take those tests. Share your findings with others – did they have you down as that sort of person with those skills?

2 Read the advice on taking psychometric tests at interview on www.bbc.co.uk/radio1/onelife

3 Draw up action plans in more detail, according to these areas of life:
   - Music
   - Money
   - Finding work
   - Personal stuff

   What are your long term and short term goals in all of these areas? Write them down. Are they achievable?

4 Take the short term goals from the above exercise and fit them into one 'Master Plan' for the next 3 – 6 months. Now change the format and use this template:

GOAL	STEPS I need to take	By WHEN?	How am I doing? TICK when done.
	1)		
	2)		
	3)		

MORE TASKS

5   Create a weekly timetable for yourself.
    You can use the pro-forma given below or make your own.

	Mon	Tue	Wed	Thurs	Fri	Sat	Sun
am							
pm							
eve							

6   Set your weekly targets in your timetable, so you make sure you allow time to achieve them!

7   Speak to your MOLP, MIC or New Deal adviser about the things that you feel are getting in the way of you achieving your goals. You might like to talk about:
    - Extra support you might be able to get on the course
    - The ADF (Adviser Discretionary Fund)
    - Other networks, groups, or help available, such as New Deal Mentoring, benefits advice or small business help.

NETWORKING

WHAT IS IT?

Networking is about meeting people who can help you in your career.

These people don't have to be 'more important' than you, or even more skilled or experienced. They might be other musicians, managers, promoters, agents, producers, film makers.

They might be people who are working in the music industry, or people like you who are on New Deal for Musicians.

Networking involves:

- understanding who you need to get to know and why
- finding out where can you get to meet these people
- getting better at communicating with people
- using networks to help you find work

WHY DO I NEED TO KNOW ABOUT THIS?

"It's not what you know, it's who you know" might be a well used phrase, but in an industry where there are few 'job adverts', it helps to know other people.

Music is a social industry and it relies largely on inter-personal and communication skills - it isn't just about being a good musician, writer or performer (although that obviously helps!).

The more people you meet who are involved with music, the more you learn from each other and make the vital contacts you need for success.

Look through the tips and case studies on any website, book or magazine and they will all refer to the people who they met who were able to move their career on.

YOU MUST HAND IN YOUR WORK BY   TO

HOW LONG
should this assignment take?

HOW
will I be assessed?

WHAT
do I do now?

Every person works at his / her own pace.
As a guide, this should take you 5 hours to read and research and another 1 hour to write your answers and discuss them with your tutor.

Your tutor will assess your work. He / she will give you feedback on how you have done. If your work needs further work to be passed, then you will be given the chance to do further work to bring it "up to scratch". For more details, please refer to your MOLP's own guidance.

Read the TASKS section below.
Then read the NOTES AND GUIDANCE section.
Carry out the TASKS.

TASKS

1 Who do you know already?
Write down everyone you know who is involved in music in some way or other. (Name of person and what do they do).
Don't include your close friends or band members (if you are in a band or in partnership with another writer or DJ).
Start with musicians, then go onto technical people and business people.

NAME
What do they do?

1	2	3	4	5
6	7	8	9	10
11	12	13	14	15
16	17	18	19	20

2 Who do you need to get to know?
Write down the people who are missing from your list and who you need to network with…

|1|2|3|4|5|

If you can only fill about 5 boxes, you urgently need to do some networking! If you can fill up all 20 boxes quite quickly, then you are already networked and are in a good position to build on your success. A good quality network can be dozens if not hundreds of people.

4 b

Through the Internet, make contact with two agencies / managers / promoters / businesses who may be able to help your music career. It's up to you what you ask them! Talk to your MOLP tutor and print out your findings or write them down here.

4 c

Through the Internet, establish your own online contact point so other people can contact you.
This might be:

e-mail address
Web site
Forum or other web presence

What is your online contact point?

5 Create an action plan which will build your network of useful contacts. (Here are a few examples to get you going, fill in the rest. Use more paper.)

WHAT TYPE of contact	HOW?
Manager	1. Ask other musicians about managers they know
	2. Look in the MMF contacts list (Music Managers forum)
Live venue	1. Look in the local paper for gig listings
	2. Ring your regional Musicians Union rep

6 What skills do you need to network? What personal skills do you need to network better? Fill in the boxes.

SKILL NEEDED	HOW I'm going to do this
example Improve telephone confidence	Phone 5 venues with a list of questions

WELL DONE, THAT'S THE END OF THIS ASSIGNMENT. CHECK IT AND HAND IT IN!

---

3 Where can you find contacts?

3 a

Talk to another musician, programmer or DJ about music, try to find out if you have any mutual friends. For instance, if they are a drummer they will probably know other bass players, who you might know as well. This is a good way of breaking the ice and discovering whether that person is already part of your network.

Write down the names and contact details of 3 other people who they have told you about

1. Name
   Contact number
   What they do

2. Name
   Contact number
   What they do

3. Name
   Contact number
   What they do

3 b

Find out about any local music networking events through your Music Industry Consultant. There will probably be at least one event near you in the next 12 months.

Write the details of the events here
– and make sure you attend!

1. Event
   Venue   Date

2. Event
   Venue   Date

3. Event
   Venue   Date

TIP

Make sure you attend and make as many contacts as possible. Remember to bring demos of your music if it's relevant. Try ringing up the PRS or the Musicians Union for details of any events.

4 Use the Internet to make new contacts

4 a

Through the Internet, make contact with 2 people who share your passion and interest for music and also share your goals for making a career in the music industry. Exchange at least 3 ideas of how you could help each other to collectively work towards your goal. Make a note of that information here or print out the information.

WHO DO YOU KNOW
ALREADY?

Make sure you recognise the value and potential of all the people you already know:
- Have you worked with other bands / DJs / musicians / programmers to promote your music together? Can they introduce you to anyone else?
- What can your contacts tell you about what works (and doesn't work) for them?
- Do your contacts know enough about your music, what your plans and ambitions are?

WHO DO YOU NEED TO
GET TO KNOW?

The music industry contains many types of people in different roles. It is important to identify the people who can help you.
Once you have met someone, you need to quickly establish whether they are a potential music contact for you.
- Do they have a role within music, or related to music such as press, media, PR?
- Do they know other people in the music industry who could be of benefit to you?

WHAT GAPS ARE THERE
IN YOUR LIST OF PEOPLE
YOU ALREADY KNOW?

- Is everyone a guitarist or singer or DJ?
- Is everyone a musician?
- Are there technical people like engineers and producers in your list?
- Are there managers, promoters and agents in your list?

Your key contacts
Amongst all the contacts you make there will be one or two people who are very important elements in the successful development of your career - musicians in a band, or a manager, agent or promoter. They need to be someone that you can trust and confide in - people that want to help build your career.
≫ Most other workbooks include information about how to get to know people who will be useful to you. Look at WORKBOOK 6, 7 and 8 in particular.

WHERE CAN YOU NETWORK?

The area that you live in may have a small music network, or it may be a city with lots of networks. You need to find out the different groups of people involved in these networks, especially ones that can have an impact on your career. Talk to your MOLP and MIC about how the music networks operate in your region.

How many times has someone said to you:

Do you know a good drummer?

Where is the best recording studio?

Where is the best club night?

Most information flow is down to **word of mouth** and you are part of that networking process.
You can use the network to its best effect by being fully inside it and knowing as many people as possible.

THESE ARE PLACES
WHERE YOU MIGHT GET TO MEET PEOPLE
WHO CAN HELP YOU:

Gigs, events, rehearsal rooms, studios, colleges, venues, MOLPs, MICs, local music networks, social events, lectures, cultural industries events in your area, potential employers and work placement employers

THIS IS
HOW YOU MIGHT LOOK FOR
THOSE PEOPLE AND PLACES:

On the Internet, using chat rooms, message boards, forums, blogs.

In your town, looking at notice boards, posters, adverts in local press and at supermarkets, going to gigs, pubs, sessions, open mic events, concerts, music shops.

Using sources of information, yellow pages, phone books, business directories, people you already know, publications and newspapers such as Loot, local press. national press, TV & radio.

 TIP

Social events like conferences, gigs and workshops / lessons are good for this.

You should have some business cards ready to give out at events.

Have your CV and portfolio ready to follow up any contact as soon as possible.
This demonstrates a willingness and enthusiasm on your part, and shows that you are quick to react. Have your CV and / or portfolio ready in three different formats: fax, e-mail, hard copy.

≫ WORKBOOK 2 shows you how to prepare a CV.

NETWORKING SKILLS

1
Be confident of
your own worth

Self-belief goes a long
way, but arrogance only
gets you so far.

2
Communicate well
with all sorts of different
people

Practice makes perfect.

3
Ask the right questions
and give the right
answers

Knowing what you want
(your action plan from
chapter 3) is the answer.

4
Give a good impression of
yourself

The way you act, dress
and use body language is
important.

5
Be yourself

People will soon find you
out if you're faking it - be
yourself. If you are polite
and easy to get on with,
it's not a problem. If you
try to pretend you know
more, you may end up
making silly mistakes and
that could cause
problems.

6
Share your network with
others

People will give you more
help if you can help them.
'Always be nice to people
when you are on the way
up as you will meet them
when you are on the way
down again'.

7
Listen carefully,
don't just talk

Always show an interest
in what the other person
is doing, rather than talk
about yourself all the
time.

If you are good at networking:

- When you meet new people, they often stay in touch with you.
- People ring you up about opportunities that come up, even if it's months later.
- People ring you up that you don't even know, because a friend has recommended you.

You need to develop your networking skills if:

- You seem to be meeting lots of people but no one is staying in contact with you.
- You find it difficult to meet new people.
- When you talk to people, the wrong words seem to come out.

You need to have some way of people catching you!
A phone number and / or an e-mail address are best.

If you haven't got an e-mail address already, then visit one of these websites and sign up for free.
It's easy to do and you can check your mail on any Internet linked computer, such as at your MOLP or library.
www.mail.yahoo.com
www.hotmail.com

BUILDING YOUR NETWORK USING INFORMATION TECHNOLOGY

WEBSITES

There are approximately 495 million people online (Nielsen Netratings - www.nielsen-netratings.com). A high proportion of surfers use the Internet to make new friends, make business acquaintances, or for want of a better phrase, network. There are many ways to meet new people online but the most popular are the use of website forums, chat rooms, newsgroups and e-mail.

The Internet is the ideal platform for introducing yourself to potential friends, new band members, managers, agencies or anyone who you get on with.

The big question is 'how do you do this'? Well it's very easy but like most things in life, there are a few ground rules you need to stick to before you join any website forum, chat rooms or newsgroups.

THE GOLDEN RULES

1.
Always read the rules and regulations for posting on that particular form or chat room. Stick to those guidelines when using the forum or chat room

2.
Always, absolutely always without fail read as many postings by a wide selection of users as possible. This will give you a good idea about the type of language used (many people use abbreviated expressions to save typing time), the general nature of the forum, room or group (aggressive, derogatory, friendly, knowledgeable, boring, useful etc) and a little insight into the characters of the people posting messages. Sometime, you can get a good idea of who you think you would get on with best before you have even communicated with them.

3.
Never ever get into a heated argument on any Internet based communication tool. If someone is provoking you then they are not worth communicating with and this type of communication only creates animosity with other users who may then not want to speak with you.

4.
Never interrupt a mid flow conversation. This is a tricky one because online conversations may have days or even weeks in between responses from one person to another. However, when you read through the postings you will be able to gauge how to initiate a conversation or introduce yourself and whether or not it is accepted practice to do so in the middle of a topic.

5.
If you have something you want to discuss with an individual member you can either invite them to a individual chat, or ask them if they would like to communicate through email or set up a new topic in the forum and invite them to join in.

6.
Never blatantly promote yourself or any products you are trying to sell on any forum, chat room or newsgroup. This of course depends upon the nature of the forum and chat room as some invite and encourage promotion. However, as a general rule of thumb, never ever use Newsgroups as a promotion tool. This is seen as an act of blatant misuse and you will more than likely be banned immediately.

7.
Remember that use of capital letters means you are shouting.

ABOUT WEBSITE FORUMS

Forums are message boards where you can leave a message and wait for someone to respond.

A website forum (sometimes called a message board) is a forum attached to a website. It's a bit like an electronic notice board. You can read messages others have left and the responses made to those messages. Or, you can start your own new topic and ask people to respond to that, or you can respond to other users messages. There can be hundreds of different topics on a large forum.

Forums are usually set up for the sole purpose to try and build an online community associated with that website. Some forums allow guests (anyone) to make a posting (leave a message or respond to a message). Others let guests read messages but not respond to any message unless you sign up to become a member (this is nearly always free and just involves you giving your name, e-mail address and some sort of nick name for use on the forum as very few people use their real name) and some forums insist you sign up before you can read or respond to postings.

If you cannot find any topics that are suitable for what you would like to discuss, you can start your own new topic. There is usually an option for you to be emailed (automatically) when someone responds to a posting you have left so you don't need to keep going back and checking the forum. If no one responds to your post, be persistent and keep trying, but bear in mind that your question has to be relevant to that forum and the type of topics being posted.

Forum examples

www.live365.com/community/
Live365 Internet Radio
- thousands of free online radio stations

http://musicians.about.com/mpboards.htm
Global musicians forum

www.ukbands.net/forum.php
UK Bands Artists Music Fans & Music Industry Promotion and Resources

ABOUT CHAT ROOMS

Chat rooms are a live area on a website where people are generally online having an active conversation with someone at that very moment.

The main benefit of chat rooms is that you can have a live chat with someone and get an immediate response because they have to be online at the same time as you to join in the chat. This is also the main disadvantage as it may not always be convenient to be online the same time as someone else. The other disadvantage is the general confusion that can be present when more than 4 or 5 people are in the same chat room at once (because a few conversations can be going on and it can be frustrating trying to type quickly to keep up).

Generally speaking, websites that have forums usually have chat rooms also for people that want to chat in real time (the term chat can be confusing, this doesn't mean you actually chat, it means you type).

ABOUT NEWSGROUPS

The most common way of accessing Newsgroups is through an e-mail client like Microsoft Outlook Express or Microsoft Entourage. There are specific Newsgroup readers that you can download (try www.download.com) and use for just reading and responding to Newsgroup postings. You can also access certain Newsgroups through your browser such as Google's Newsgroups (groups.google.com).

Newsgroups are a vast source of information and a great way of making direct contact with people that share your interests and passions, but because of the nature of this communication platform it can be worthwhile carefully researching your chosen Newsgroup before you ask to join in. They can also be a little tricky to get used to.

A full explanation of Newsgroups is beyond the scope of this document, but you can find out more information online at http://groups.google.com or you could try searching the Internet for a "Newsgroup beginners guide".

If you would like to set up your e-mail client to read Newsgroups you'll need to search the Internet for instructions on how to do this for your e-mail client. For example, if you are using Microsoft Outlook Express, then you could type the following into a search engine "Microsoft outlook express reading newsgroups".

ABOUT BLOGS

Blogs are a way of setting up your own web page in the form of a personal diary where you can leave a daily or weekly account of what you've been up to or whatever you want. They have been around since about 1998 and every year become more and more popular. Visitors to your website blog can comment on your postings or link to them or email you directly if you have an email address. Blogs do not suit everyone but if you are an emerging band they are a great way for fans to keep in touch.

Best of all you need absolutely no technical experience to set up a blog and it's free. A complete explanation and set of instructions are beyond the scope of this book, but everything you need to know can be read here (www.blogger.com).

Good look with your blog!

SUMMARY

Learning to use this new communication tools can be frustrating and even a little nerve racking for the Internet newby, but persistence pays off and in time you can make some life long friends and very valuable contacts. Remember, practice makes perfect.

WANT TO KNOW MORE?

LINKS

New Deal for Musicians has no responsibility for or control of the following sites. The inclusion of any site does not necessarily imply New Deal for Musicians approval of the site. To access any of the sites please type in the address into a browser or search using keywords from the name of the link. www.dfes.gov.uk/ukonlinecentres Find Internet access that's close to you.

GENRE BASED SITES / NETWORKING

☐ **www.jazzservices.org.uk**
Jazz Services
The national service organisation for jazz in the UK. Contains free fact sheets on subjects such as manufacturing Cds, marketing your gig plus lots of jazz information and news, including gig listings.

☐ **www.banditnewsletter.com**
Bandit. A+R subscription site and publication.

☐ **www.songlink.com**
Opportunities for networking.

☐ **www.ukdj.org**
An Organisation for DJs based in the UK. Sections on local charts, DJ rosters and offering commercial services such as marketing There are music and creative industries networks across the UK – search the Internet using keywords 'music', 'network' 'creative industries' 'UK' or your own keywords.

☐ **www.tgcsp.org.uk**
Thames Gateway Creative Skills Partnership. Resources and links for individuals and organisations involved in the business of creative learning and enterprise, based in London but many links are applicable UK wide.

☐ **www.manchester-music.org.uk**
Manchester City Music Network works to strengthen and develop the infrastructure of the music industry in Manchester and offers training.

☐ **www.artsnetworks.net**
support organisations list across UK, quite limited but worth a look

☐ **www.cids.co.uk**
interactive portal for creative industries businesses in Manchester.

TIP

These are only a few examples!
The best way to find websites which work for you is to search yourself. Use the information in chapter 2 to help you do this!

MUSIC WEBZINES (ONLINE - MAGAZINES)

☐ www.djzone.net
webzine for the professional DJ.

☐ www.metalliville.com
Metalliville. Artist interviews, CD and show
reviews, and general information about the
heavy metal scene in the UK.

☐ www.rawroots.co.uk
Raw Roots. Dedicated to underground and
independent hip hop in the U.K. and across the
globe.

☐ www.fly.co.uk
Fly Magazine. Jazz, hip hop, R&B, dance and
indie music from around the world.

☐ www.bigmouth.co.uk
Bigmouth. U.K. music information with tour
dates, music events, and artist information.

☐ www.danceportalglobal.com
DancePortalGlobal. global dance music and
clubbing events. includes listings, reviews,
competitions, and audio / video webcasts.

☐ www.thesituation.co.uk
The Situation. Features U.S. and U.K. garage,
rap, and soul music news including interviews,
videos, reviews, and more.

☐ www.fusedmagazine.com
Fused Magazine. Covering the cream of the
underground music scene in the U.K. Features
record, club, video, film, and event reviews and
interviews.

BOOKS

☐ Musicians Bible 2002 :
Complete Guide to the Music Business
Collis, John
Publisher : Penguin Books
ISBN : 0140295682

☐ Networking in the Music Business
Kimpel, Dan, Sally Englefried (Editor)
Publisher : Artistpro.com
ISBN : 0872887278

☐ Music Week – Music Week Directory 2004
Publisher : CMP Information
ISBN : 0863825532

☐ MCR : Music – The Unsigned Guide,
North West
Stephen D.M. Loukes, Lee F. Donnelly
Publisher : mcr : music
ISBN : 0954460103

MORE TASKS

1 Read WORKBOOK 6 – CHAPTER 2, WORKBOOK 7 – CHAPTER 1 and WORKBOOK 8 – CHAPTER 1. Who do you need to add to your network?

2 Join at least 2 newsgroups or forums which are relevant to you.

3 Write up your 'little black book' of contacts. Ask people for theirs and offer yours. Don't keep those scraps of paper and business cards without making a note somewhere else as well.

4 Find a 'soulmate' who will go places with you so you don't feel alone… but not allow you to just talk to them all night.

5 Travel to your nearest networking session run by:
MU / MMF / or local music organisations. Examples include goNORTH, In the City and come away with a load of contacts to follow up.

6 Broaden your horizons by going to meetings with people on the periphery – film makers; visual artists; drama based organisations;

7 Go to support sessions organised by network organisations e.g. MCMN, PANDA, CIDS, etc Get help from your MIC or MOLP to find out the network organisations in your area.

8 Investigate networks through business link. (www.businesslink.org.uk)

9 Build your networking skills – enrol on a course in interpersonal skills, communication, psychology, sign language or painting portraits – all new networking experiences help.

ACKNOWLEDGEMENTS

These materials have been developed by ARMSTRONG LEARNING, working with City College Manchester.
Art direction and design by LULU BUTTERFLY
Cover photograph by Ray Chan

NEW DEAL FOR MUSICIANS
THE MUSIC INDUSTRY AND YOU

Special thanks go to all who have contributed to the development of the workbooks including:
The New Deal for Musicians Steering Group
The Open Learning Materials Steering Group
Department for Education and Skills
Teacher Training Agency
All those who have contributed to the case studies.
Music Open Learning Providers and Music Industry Consultants who have piloted the materials.
Sound Advice

MU	Musicians' Union
MPG	Music Producers Guild
AIM	Association of Independent Music
PRS	Performing Right Society
MCPS	Mechanical - Copyright Protection Society
MMF	Music Managers Forum
BPI	British Phonographic Industry
MPA	Music Publishers Association
PPL / VPL	Phonographic Performance Limited / Video Performance Limited
MIA	Music Industries Association
PAMRA	Performing Artists' Media Rights Association

BBC Radio 1
British Music Rights
British Academy of Composers and Songwriters